FIRST STEPS
IN FAMILY HISTORY

GUIDED BY EVE McLAUGHLIN

COUNTRYSIDE BOOKS
NEWBURY, BERKSHIRE

Other Genealogy Titles available from Countryside Books include:

FURTHER STEPS IN FAMILY HISTORY
Eve McLaughlin

BEGINNING YOUR FAMILY HISTORY
George Pelling

TRACING YOUR ANCESTORS: THE A–Z GUIDE
Pauline Saul

First Published 1989
© Eve McLaughlin 1989
Second edition 1992
Third edition 1995

COUNTRYSIDE BOOKS
3 Catherine Road
Newbury, Berkshire

ISBN 1 85306 061 5

Produced through MRM Associates Ltd., Reading
Typeset by Acorn Bookwork, Salisbury
Printed in England

CONTENTS

INTRODUCTION

The Pleasure of Their Company

Finding out something about your ancestors is a fascinating business, which can add a whole new dimension to your life. And, because your ancestors provided the fabric from which you are built, it may lead you to a greater knowledge of yourself and your capabilities. It can give you useful warnings of trouble to come. Great-great-uncle Jim lost his temper and thumped the farm bailiff in 1830, lost his job, so stole a sheep to feed his hungry family, and got transported to Australia. You don't get on with the sales manager – but if you really come to blows (even metaphorical) with him, he may take revenge. Do you sincerely want to be transferred to the sales office in Uttar Pradesh? (Or Down Under even?)

But seriously, for most of us, the days are gone when we live where our forefathers had lived for generations. We can no longer walk round the streets in the comfortable knowledge that our grandfather passed the same house daily on his way to work or the pub; the local church-yard is not full of our ancestors' tombstones, nor can we drop in at the little house round the corner and ask Grandpa or Aunt Fanny what sort of person was great-great-uncle

Jedediah Bloggs
A Godly example
to Sinners and
Backsliders.

(A pain in the rear?) If we want to find out about our ancestors, not just their names and dates, but what kind of people they were and what sort of lives they led, it takes time and dedication.

However, with a little bit of homework first, it is possible to avoid most of the time-consuming mistakes and go straight to the right places for the right information at the right time. So much help is now available in all directions that it is a pity not to take advantage of it. It still isn't press-a-button-and-out-it-all-comes, which would be pretty boring any-way. But press the right button at the right time, and you will get the hot coffee you wanted, instead of the cold tea flavoured with oxtail soup. Everyone's ancestors have a lot of similarities, so that the routes towards tracing them coincide. This volume is largely concerned with taking the first steps on those routes and establishing a good basis for further research in the more complex and diverse records.

Eve McLaughlin 1992

NO TIME FOR FAMILY HISTORY?

People often say 'That sounds interesting, but I haven't time to do it now. Perhaps when I'm retired.' But they find that when they have retired, a lot of the best sources of information – the family – are dead and regret those missed opportunities. To avoid this, I start with something which those with the bare minimum of time can do, now.

Be prepared for surprises, for skeletons even – they are the exciting bits. But even the most 'ordinary' family is fascinating to trace, because the way of life which made them 'ordinary' in their own time is now so far from our present day living as to be exotic in itself. You will be constantly amazed at how they managed with so little, or wasted so much; twelve children in two bedrooms, or twelve servants for two people. You will share their sorrows and joys, thrill at their small triumphs, pity their defeats. It is all there, in the records, waiting to be discovered, by you, about your own people. And it's a lot of fun finding out.

Do I just trace my father's family?

There are no rules about what you can and cannot do. You are a mixture of all the ancestors on your father's side and your mother's. The old-fashioned idea was that male ancestry mattered most, and a family with no sons had 'died out'. That is peculiar, but so perhaps, is the insistence on tracing from mother to grandmother only, on the grounds that no one can be sure who the father of a child is.

On the whole, it is simplest to assume that a child of a married woman is her husband's – which is English law – unless you have remarkably solid evidence to the contrary. It is best to trace both, or all, sides of the family if possible, since they are part of your make-up. If you are short of time, then start on the one with the least common name, or most accessible records. I have assumed for the sake of argument that the typical reader of this book happens to have a fairly uncommon surname, which we will call Bloggs, because it really is uncommon.

But I have also allowed for the person whose father's surname was Smith, who would probably find it easier to cut his teeth on his mother's name. Nothing is impossible, for I was once asked to trace John Smith, born on a stated (slightly wrong) date in Essex, with the only details his occupation and a garbled version of his employer's name. I found him and took that family back to 1620, but it isn't an exercise I would recommend to a beginner. Everyone has something going for them, and if you make the best of every clue offered, you too can have a family like John Smith's.

I haven't got the time

A lot of people think they haven't got time to do this or that – they work full time, are tied to the house with babies, aged parents, dogs, gerbils – but if they really want to, they can make time. Having the desire to do something is the key to the problem, and the fact that you have bought this book, or are even considering buying it now, means you have the desire – why not give in to temptation and make your dreams come true? Some people are going to have more trouble finding time, but this book should enable them to take a few short cuts, and make the most of what time they have got.

First, the difficulties.

Working nine to five

This is a problem, because it seems that all the official repositories also work nine to five. When you get down to it, a number of them have weekly or bi-weekly evening openings, or some Saturday mornings. There are often copies of some of the things you need, in places which are open out of office hours. If you know what you need, you can get photostats for much less than it would have cost to go there and see the originals.

Do you spend your lunchtime in the pub and the afternoon wishing you hadn't? Can you drop into your local library instead? There is a wealth of information to be obtained, either from books you can borrow, or through reading reference books while you are there. A good reference library has a great deal of information about the past as well as the present, about all parts of the country or world, not just the local area.

There will be copies of most of the standard genealogical textbooks –

my own guides; the Gibson series which tell you where to find particular types of records and what years survive: special books on tracing, e.g. Scottish, Welsh or Irish ancestors, Quakers, Baptists, soldiers, sailors, merchant navy men, gentry families, combmakers etc etc. What they haven't got on the shelves, they can get from other libraries for you. Some information is on microfiche, which they may have. If not, it is cheap enough to buy it yourself and read on the library fiche reader.

If you are lucky enough to live in the area where your ancestors came from, you should be able to see particular documents or books in a snatched half hour or so, at the local Record Office or library, provided you make arrangements in advance and order what you need to be ready for you the minute you arrive. The kind of things you can expect to see are detailed later on.

Then there are holidays. Would you rather spend three weeks on the Costa Packet, getting sunburn and embarrassing intestinal ailments, or have some time to get acquainted with the place your ancestors came from? There are long weekends too, to try the experiment first. If you can contact any relatives 'out of hours', either nearby or on these trips, they may be able to give you quite a lot of information, between them, which will build into quite a respectable family tree and form the basis for work in official sources.

I've got small children so I can't get out

I do sympathise, having brought up four myself. It isn't the actual housework so much, given modern equipment, as the lack of reasonable lengths of time you can call your own. Babies are not programmed to switch on and off to order; toddlers need constant watching and teaching. The only comfort is, the better you do it, the sooner you will be in the clear. Once they go to school, or even nursery school, you do have a few hours of time which can be turned to good account.

The sooner children learn that Mother has interests of her own, the better. Left to himself, the child will assume the world revolves around him, and demand total devotion to his needs. From provider of food, nurse and mopper-upper for the tinies, you will become personal slave to the older ones. It is good for them to learn to cook, clear up and find their own socks, against the day you walk under a bus/run off with the milkman. (On second thoughts, I take that back. Socks have a life of their own and may need the whole family mobilised to track them down.) Your personal hobby will carry you through the 'empty nest' syndrome which affects the maternal slave when they find another lasagne-maker and sock-detective.

There is a surprising amount you can do in odd half-hours at home, by correspondence. You can borrow books from the library, and ask for any titles mentioned in the bibliography at the back. The staff should be able to suggest other books which they can get for you, from elsewhere.

Drop in there for an hour or so and study the reference books which can't be borrowed – anything could be useful.

Any nearby relatives can be tapped for family knowledge – even those you don't normally get on with may come through if you get them to tell you about their past lives, rather than about the nasty neighbours or the cost of tea-bags. Ask for addresses of other relatives and write to them.

Weekend trips can be changed from quarrelsome afternoons on the crowded beach or sitting in a traffic jam on the motorway, to visiting distant places or relatives to gain more ancestral knowledge. Holidays can be manipulated in the same way – less expensive, less banal, less predictable.

If you are allowed out in the evening, you could go to classes in tracing your ancestors, and you may be able to team up with someone else with the same interests and ties, so that you can stagger care of children and searching. At least, if you can achieve limited freedom, and make one trip to the General Register Office, someone else may be able to do some of your leg-work for you by collecting certificates.

When you are almost ready, build yourself up some Brownie points by baby-sitting for friends in a similar position and take out the 'credit' by getting one or several of them to take charge of your family for a whole day. That way, you can get to London, or one of the other centres with official information, and advance your knowledge. Don't squander the credit too early to be able to use the time to the full – unless you have very accommodating friends. A reliable home bird, who loves staying in the kitchen and cooking for your little angels is well worth cultivating when you are tied.

Tied by disablement

If you are personally disabled, then actually getting into strange places is often the problem. If you are wheelchair-bound, always enquire first about access to the library or other repository. There are quite a lot of ramps at entrances now, or, if the staff know to expect you, they can take you up in lifts or get a porter to heft the chair. There is usually someone around who can help with the trickier manoeuvres. Check up on the loo situation, and if it is on a different floor, try to go when you are passing it, not make the helper go back on his tracks right away. Make your handicap work for you by getting them to bend the rules – after all, they were made with rough able-bodied users in mind, and you have an angelic touch.

If you have arthritis, this can be awkward, since most Record Offices make you use pencils, which need stronger grip and pressure than pens. You could perhaps take an assistant to write things down: or dictate quietly into a tape recorder for transcription at home. Both will involve talking, not usually encouraged in a Record Office, so ask in advance and they may put you in a separate corner.

You may have found that it is easier to use a word processor than a typewriter. There are genuinely portable battery-powered word processors available on which you can key in your notes and transfer the disk to your main WP when you get home. Of course, you would need permission to use one, but most Record Offices now give this. The Public Record Office allows typewriters, which are much noisier than the modern 'silent' keyboards.

I'm tied by another's disability

If you are a full-time carer, then most of your work will be done by correspondence or via library loans. However, if your charge is physically but not mentally handicapped, is it possible to rearrange the house so that everything needed for two hours is within reach? A feeling of independence is good for the patient too. If necessary, perhaps someone else would come and just sit by – a lot of people will help if they are only asked, and given precise instructions. There may be a Day Centre which will take the patient for a few hours. You are not neglecting your charge, since a break for you will help you cope better otherwise.

What can I do by post?

A great deal of progress can be made through writing letters, and that only needs an odd half hour to start. Your known close relatives are the first target, since they may know a surprising amount. For what to ask them, see 'Interviewing Elderly Relatives'. They may be able to give you some addresses of dim and distant aunties or tell you where the family once lived.

The library is a good source of addresses too. First, the larger ones will, the smaller ones may, have a national set of phone books; the book for the ancestral area should have people of 'your' name. If your surname is at all uncommon, then any phone book could be tried for examples. How do you decide what *is* uncommon? Count up the number appearing in phone books – if you find a lot in one place but never more than ten in others, that's pretty rare. Be prepared to take alternative spellings, though, since your grandfather may have turned peculiar.

Addresses of people actually interested in tracing their ancestors can be found in several publications. Quite a lot of libraries have the international Genealogical Research Directory, published in Australia, which has a lot of overseas researchers but plenty of British ones too. Besides, one of those Australians could well be your long-lost cousin and have letters from your own great-grandfather. This 'GRD' has been published for several years, and there was also a National Research Directory, published in Sussex, which is very similar. Every Family History Society (see later) publishes lists of its own members' interests, and probably your local library will have at least the local FHS list. Don't pass this by if your ancestors came from somewhere else – so did those of a lot of other people included.

Family Tree Magazine (FTM) which is published every month, regularly includes a list of ancestral names researched by readers, and you can have yours included for a small fee. If your name does turn out to be unusual, it is pretty certain that one of the other bearers will be doing a One Name Study on it. This means collecting every possible entry of the name, including every one in the index at St Catherine's (see later), a list of wills, phone book entries etc. Your library may have the Register of the Guild of One Name Studies ('Goons') or you can buy it for about £3 from the Society of Genealogists. It could save you a lot of time if you write to the registered researcher.

If you do write to a stranger (or even distant kin), you will need to give to get – establish your bona fides by explaining first who you are. At all costs, avoid saying 'I want to know all about the Bloggses'. The reaction is 'Why? What is he/she up to?' Or, if the person knows a lot, 'When I have six months to spare'. For possibles in the ancestral area – call it Handley – try something like:

I am John Richard Bloggs, born in 1942, I am a computer programmer, married to Carol, two children etc etc. My father was George Bloggs, who died last year aged 72. He was born in Handley and was a carpenter at first, with his uncle Harry, in Heatherby, till the war. He joined up in 1940, and when he was stationed near London, he met my mother Ruby Jane Crompton. They got married in 1941 and I was born in Lewisham. My mother and I moved out to Wiltshire, where my brother Andrew and my sister Linda were born. After the war, we settled in Brighton. I gather his father was called Andrew too, and he was a plumber. Somebody kept a pub called the Three Feathers and there was another uncle called Barty.

There is enough there for them to recognise father as young Georgie, who went off to live in foreign parts and was never heard of again. Locally-living people should be able to fill in details of grandfather Andrew, to tell you that he married Ellie or Allie, the sister of Bartholomew Jardine who kept the 'Prince of Wales'. That gives you a new surname to think about.

For the bearers of the name in a different area, probably details of your wife and family are not relevant for the first approach. Start with 'I am the son of George Bloggs (1916–1988) born in Handley' etc. The name Andrew is sufficiently distinctive to be identifiable.

Even if they don't recognise the names, ask them to tell you about their father, grandfather, brothers and sisters etc. Maybe you don't know the names yet, but further researches could show they are descended from a cousin or uncle of Andrew. Or maybe one of your other correspondents will turn out to be related to that one – in which case, you can put them in touch and perhaps start a friendship chain going.

The GOONS will want that sort of detail too – if you say George was born on 14 August 1916, the researcher should already have a record of the registration quarter (not a certificate) and possibly of a marriage of Andrew fifteen years or so before. If another Bloggs has enquired about the same line, they will put you in touch. Some One Namers are organised into a family association and issue a newsletter.

Remember, always, always, send an SAE. But do not think that this gives you a right to a reply by return, or, indeed, at all. You are asking for help, and for personal information, and must be prepared to wait for it. In some cases, the more people know, the longer they are going to take to sort out what is relevant to you. They may be old and short-sighted, and have to wait till our Mary comes round even to read the letter, never mind reply. They may be away on holiday, ill, or very busy when the letter arrives. A lot of mail is delayed or vanishes entirely. After several months, a polite enquiry to make sure it arrived is in order, a peremptory demand for instant response isn't. If the matter is urgent, phone, politely.

Use the power of the Press

Failing anyone in the ancestral area phone book (especially if the surname is too common for letters to other areas to be sensible), why not write to the local paper? You could advertise, but who reads through all the small ads? Write a letter to the Editor, and if you have enough identifiable details, he will probably print it, in which case you could hear from Harry's daughter Elsie, now in her 70s. If your original letter produces much extra information, write to thank them, repeating enough of the details to catch the eye of another group of readers.

If there seems to be an interesting story, some journalist may even follow it up for you. But beware of reviving old scandals which they may print the next week. You may think it hilarious that Uncle Jethro was the town drunk, or habitually wandered the streets in women's dress reading the Bible to passers-by. His spinster daughters still living in the neighbourhood won't.

Some radio stations already run a 'where are they now?' feature and others might if you suggested it. Write to them, and be ready for a phone call asking for details – they may be taping it or even transmitting live, so iron out the 'er, ums' and 'his name was – now let me see, Harry, no I tell a lie, that was the other one, er, I think he was, um, Jim. John? . . .'

Writing to 'ancestral' libraries

Assuming you don't live in the place your ancestors came from, how can you make any progress? There is a great deal of information about the area, perhaps even about your family, held in the main reference library there. Couldn't they just copy it out and send it to you? Well, no.

Libraries are for providing and caring for books, attending to readers, who are local ratepayers, and only as a concession for searching for and sending out information by post to outsiders.The latest government directive is that they charge for anything which takes longer than a few minutes.

However, it would be entirely reasonable to ask whether your great-grandfather's name and street address appears in a local directory of about 1881 (normally only if he was rich or a tradesman in his own right) and also if he was there in 1871. It wouldn't be reasonable to ask them to extract all the Bloggs entries in any directories they have. Some librarians might be good enough to go beyond what was asked and send you a photostat of the half-page advertisement for the firm. Some might really put themselves out and look out that 1881 address in the 1881 census they have on microfilm and send you the entry – but even with an address, that isn't a two-minute job, unless they have a good street or surname index provided by the local Family History Society. It is not a service you can demand, and if it is provided, be lavishly grateful.

Many county or borough libraries have Local Studies departments, with a lot of manuscript or typescript material, maps and filmed material as well as printed books. Sometimes they have copies of the local parish registers too. The librarians in charge are often very knowledgeable indeed about the area, and can suggest books for you to borrow through the Central Lending system, or make photostat copies of parts of typescripts etc (for which you would expect to pay). They can also tell you where places are or were – e.g. Sebastopol Villas was where the Tesco supermarket is now and number 6 was somewhere near the bacon counter.

Writing to County Record Offices

County, or City, Record Offices (CROs) are where most of the parish registers and other manuscript archive material are kept nowadays, so they have a great deal of information about your ancestors. Once they were quiet backwaters, where few people penetrated and the arrival of a letter was a welcome diversion. They would answer queries happily and usually freely. Things have changed – people pour in looking for their ancestors, letters come in shoals, and the pressures from local authorities are for making the service pay. So far, only three offices charge for personal searchers, but postal enquirers are sometimes asked to pay a set charge or a 'donation'.

They should answer for no cost straightforward questions about whether they hold parish registers and for which years; if not, where are they?; what other records are available which cover a parish, a manor or a trade; if they have a will for a named person at a stated date. They will also usually check if one baptism or marriage is there in a named parish, but they won't extract 'all the Bloggs entries in Handley' free. That is usually about it, though they may do half an hour's personal work and request a donation.

This is because their main job is to care for and repair registers and other items and make them available under supervision to people who come to the office. Most of the material they hold is in unindexed manuscripts and takes time to get out of the storeroom and read. Sometimes they send a list of local record searchers, sometimes they appoint one of their own (charging well over the odds for this, since 'overheads' are levied as well as the standard fee per hour).

They should be able to send you photostats of wills and other single documents – and sometimes of known individual entries in registers, though not all offices will copy bound books. They won't usually find and photostat entries of unknown date. However, some offices have funny rules about a minimum charge for the service, and it costs as much for one page as for six, so enquire first.

Most of them have a leaflet for enquirers which includes their rules of operation. Read this carefully, since you will be deemed to be acting on what it says. If you get a sudden opportunity to visit, it is best to phone, and some CROs demand it. If it says 'advance booking is advised' that means you might get in unexpectedly. 'Advance booking is necessary' means they could turn you away even if the search room was empty.

Writing to the local vicar

Grandpa was born in Handley, why not ask the vicar to copy down all the Bloggs entries in his registers? Send him a stamped addressed envelope, of course, because vicars aren't paid much.

In the first place, most parish registers are now in the County Record Office (CRO). By law, all those over a hundred years old should be, unless very special provisions have been made, to protect these irreplaceable records from vandals, fire, damp, careless handling and loss. So most clergy have only got the registers currently in use.

In the second place, even if they have the registers, they probably can't read the older writing and, as very busy men, they tend to take a horrified glance and say there are no Bloggs entries there, even if there are.

A request for a single baptism might come free, and if more is sent, a 'donation' is reasonable. But beware of asking for 'everything' without asking for a quotation. Clergy are entitled to charge for access to registers in the parish and if they also do researching, they tend to charge professional fees on top of that, for very amateur work. Some don't, but some demand a great deal.

What the vicar may be able to tell you is if there are still people named Bloggs in the village (though not everyone attends church and he may not know them) and, importantly, if there is a parish historian, who knows all about the village. It may be a churchwarden, who could be (illegally) in charge of the registers if held, but quite probably such a person will have a typed copy of the registers, maps and a lot of other material, including oral history of the village. If they will help you, you can do very well. Again, a donation towards the good work should be offered tactfully – photostats, card indexes, computer storage, all cost money.

Writing to professional organisations or firms

If you know your ancestor was in one of the professions, held a particular office or worked for a known firm, there may be information to be got. First, of course, check with your local library, to see if they have a printed directory of people who were e.g. doctors, vets, dentists, clergymen, railway engineers in the past. If not, then ask for the current address of the professional body concerned, and write to them.

Almost all professional organisations have an archivist or librarian, who will be prepared to assist with any information they hold about your man. It may not be a lot – just the fact that he did operate in a certain area at a certain date – but for some people, there will be more. Nonconformist churches do have archivists and details about their clergy, especially good obituaries, but the Church of England, which has been going rather longer, would refer you to printed works about clergymen who were university graduates, or *Crockford's Clerical Directory* from 1858. Senior clergy are well covered in the *Dictionary of National Biography*.

Large old-established firms may have a librarian/archivist at their headquarters (ask the library) or just a personnel or pensions department with a few old files in the basement. Some old firms have had histories written. If the person you are chasing could still be alive, you will have to prove your identity and right to ask. There may be photographs of old employees who worked long enough for the gold watch – but more of the managers than the tea lady. However, women 'doing a man's job' were often photographed extensively.

If you are writing because the name and trade of the firm is the same as your ancestor's, you may find that no one now in management still has that name, because it was sold in 1920. Check in *Who Owns Whom* at the library. But the firm may have an address for the old owner's grandson, who has family knowledge.

If your ancestor was supposed to be e.g. Mayor of Little Puddle in 1902, first check with the area library to make sure. A directory of the date lists all officials, and will show if he was only a councillor or town clerk. The current office holder, or more likely some council dogs-body, should be able to confirm this, and maybe tell you something about him and whether there is a portrait in the Town Hall.

If you are going to do a lot of writing around, then a cheap typewriter bought through the second-hand columns of the local paper is practically a must. Anyone can learn to type slowly with a little experimentation – you don't need classes or a genius I.Q. The reason is that unless you have truly remarkable print-style handwriting, some of your correspondents will find it difficult to read. I regularly get pages of close-packed scrawl which take me ages to decipher – and I'm supposed to be a handwriting expert. I defy anyone to read my own writing if I'm in a hurry, so I know what I'm talking about. The easier it is to read, the more likely people are to try to answer. If you must write by hand, then print all names of people and places and use dark ink.

Just an odd couple of hours out here and there

1. Your local library
If you are limited to your own local area for most of your searches, then – apart from the family – the local library is going to be your life-line. If you happen to live in your ancestral area, you are very lucky, and can do a lot of the things described later in this book. If you are in the Greater London area, many sources are open to you. But for the moment, I will assume that you are not living in your ancestral area, and not in London. Do not despair.

Most libraries have a lot of books you can borrow and take home – or they can get them for you through the Central Lending system from a library at the other end of the country which stocks them. There are specifically genealogical works, mentioned in this book, some of which are cheap enough to buy, others really only accessible through a library. There are printed parish registers, mostly published in the last century when it was cheaper, but a few more recently by Family History Societies (FHSs).

There just might be a book about your family. Don't be led into buying one of the alleged 'family history books' published by an American firm in Ohio, who have been circularising persons in England recently, having shifted their operation from America to Canada to Australia earlier. The books, alleged to have been written by Richard C . . . or Harold G . . . (fill in your own surname), have a few very basic general hints on how you can trace your own ancestors, with some very out-of-date addresses to write to, plus a list of entries from old American and English telephone directories, which you could get yourself at the library. Just send £15 and you too can be disappointed.

Genuine books about families do exist, and the respectable ones can be borrowed first to see if they are what they claim. There are three books in most reference libraries, usually shelved together, called *The Genealogist's Guide* (G. Marshall 1903), *A Genealogical Guide* (J. B. Whitmore, covers 1903–53) and the *Genealogist's Guide* 1953–1975 (G. Barrow) and sometimes T. Thompson's *British Family Histories in Print* (with an appendix covering 1975–80). These cover all printed pedigrees of three or more male generations.

However, these are mostly of well-to-do families and sometimes only consist of half a page. The guides don't have actual pedigrees, but a list of other books, with volume and page, where they will be found. If your library has Fax, it can locate the book and get you a copy of the page, often in quite a short time, for a small cost.

Never seize on a famous person or a gentry family with a name like yours and try to tack yourself on to it. Always work back from yourself, from what you know to what you don't know. People called Shakespeare can't be descended from William – he had one son who died, and his married daughters' descendants petered out. If great-grandfather was called John Wesley Smith, it doesn't show he was related, just that his family were good Methodists. If there is a rumour of such a relationship in the family, and the story can't be traced back to Auntie Flo who used to spend her life reading romances, you still need to work back from you, but just maybe it is right, even if many centuries further back than you imagine.

More likely to be useful to you (unless you *are* from a wealthy family) would be the articles about families printed in the magazines of Family History Societies. Your library will probably have the local FHS magazine, and maybe those of neighbouring counties, and there is a list of abstracts of which articles are in which FHS magazine in the *Family History News and Digest* published every six months. However, the easiest way to get access to all these magazines is by joining your local FHS. Remember that articles about Lancashire families could be printed in the Devon or Bucks magazines, because a local member sent them in.

Try to read as much as possible about the place your ancestors lived in, the trade they followed and the general social history of the times. A lot of books have been written covering a particular trade, and some of them are so detailed that they actually mention names. Even comparatively humble callings are not neglected. Victorian farm labourers, domestic servants, washerwomen, straw plaiters, chain makers, shepherds, all have their literature. Each county had a study of farming done in the early 1800s, and you might be able to read what Farmer Bloggs planted then and what his yields were. Knowledge about the past will stand you in good stead in interviewing old people and in making sense of what you discover in official records.

Local libraries also have many reference books to professions, classes and trades – not necessarily on the open shelves. If you are interested in American landscape artists of the last century, ask if they have such a book in their reserve stock. You may be the only person who has asked since 1921, so they shifted it downstairs, but didn't throw it away. If they haven't got it, they may know a man who has.

The largest provincial reference libraries do set out to stock material from all counties, because they know their local residents come from all over. Printed parish registers, county histories, runs of volumes produced by county record societies, reference books done by county, like the growing series of books about clock and watchmakers, indexes of wills, directories of other areas, books about localised trades – generally, a close study of the shelves reveals totally unexpected riches.

These days, most reference libraries have a lot of material on microfilm or microfiche. Some of it will refer to the local county only. For instance, copies of the local censuses are pretty widespread, and some libraries have copy parish registers, old newspapers etc. But there is usually microfilm of national reference material, and genealogical tools like the IGI (see below under Mormon libraries) and some data for adjacent counties. Census districts in particular may span county boundaries. Your county will have a few parishes over the county line. At the very least, you can have a look at a census and see what it is like, against the time when you can use one for yourself.

Newspapers also have a lot of news from adjacent counties, and major crimes will get a good write-up all over the place. You can read about the 'orrible murder in Manchester or the first Great Train Robbery in the comfort of your library hundreds of miles away. Old newspapers are a good read anyway, because of the background information provided about the way people were living then. A bad winter, a good harvest, cheap foreign imports, new railway services or a craze for riding bicycles might have an impact anywhere.

2. The Mormon library

The Church of Latter Day Saints (LDS or Mormons) has opened a number of libraries all over the country, initially for their own members, who are obliged to trace their ancestors and baptise them into the church retrospectively. However, they have extended the use of these libraries to the public, as Family History Centres, and if you happen to have one near you, this is very convenient. There is a list on page 58. Some are open all the time, some only for one afternoon or evening a week, so you will need to phone first. You won't get pressured to join, unless you express an interest.

What they provide is access to a wide range of British family history material, on microfilm, for a small hire charge per film of £1.45. In most libraries, there is a small stock and the rest is on order from America, which may take some weeks, so preliminary enquiries are vital.

They can obtain any census films; parish registers (not all, but a lot); some of the St Catherine's indexes (see later); some wills; some Scottish material; some Irish material; and a mass of miscellaneous films. Each Mormon library has a catalogue of what can be ordered, so you may need a brief visit to consult this and a longer research visit weeks later. Obviously, if someone else has been using the film you need, it might be there right away, since it is kept for a few weeks once arrived.

The libraries will also have the International Genealogical Index (IGI), a collection of baptisms and marriages, computer-sorted county by county into surname order. This isn't much use till you are back into the last century, since there are few entries after 1875, and in some places not many after about 1840. Once you get there, it can be a handy short-cut to locating possible ancestors. It isn't complete or 100% accurate, so you will at some stage have to check up on it, especially by searching burials, to make sure the ancestor you have picked out didn't die aged 10. It is, however, a useful aid and a splendid guide to which counties particular surnames were common in.

A Family Registry is kept by the LDS church, listing the names and addresses of persons researching particular families or surnames. You can add your name to this at the Mormon Library or by writing to the Genealogical Department in Salt Lake City (see addresses).

3. Adult education classes
There may be an afternoon adult education class in family history. Check with your local centre, or the library will have information. They usually start in September, but sometimes there are short courses in spring or summer as well.

I can only get out in the evenings or weekends

Libraries are open some evenings a week and usually on Saturdays. Relatives are accessible then, especially if you have the use of a car. Evening classes in tracing your ancestors are held all over the country.

Family History Societies tend to meet in the evenings during the week or on Saturday afternoons. I strongly recommend you to track down your local one (via the library) and join it and perhaps the ancestral area one as well. There is a Society for almost every county, for many cities and for some smaller locations. Some have a number of small branches, if there are large towns in their area, and some have 'house groups' or special interest groups. For instance, several FHSs have a computer group; Manchester has a local Scottish group; Bucks has local groups of members with Yorkshire, West Country and Scottish ancestors; Dorset has a London-based group and Cornwall an Australian branch.

Normally, there will be regular monthly meetings, in one or different venues, with a talk by an expert, or in the smaller groups, just for discussions among members. You can exchange experiences, get advice, buy cheap guides and recording stationery and generally get together with like-minded people, some of whom will become fast friends. No one expects you to know it all right away, or to have gentry ancestors or even respectable ancestors. FHS members love a sheep stealer (well, in retrospect).

Each Society has a library, of general genealogical books, local county material and increasing amounts from other counties. There is also an exchange of magazines between the various FHSs, and normally you can borrow any of this material to read at home. You can read magazines from the ancestral area, and decide whether to join that FHS as well. Don't be too precipitate in picking an ancestral place. Sometimes you will discover that your Yorkshire ancestors went there in 1845 or your 'definitely London' ancestors didn't get there till 1890, perhaps from some totally surprising place. I've known people settle in the very county their ancestors left a hundred years back. One person even bought the house next door to the ancestral home, without the slightest notion.

All FHSs are doing something towards making their local records more available, by transcribing registers and censuses, printing them, whole or as indexes, copying tombstone inscriptions and any other lists or records of people they can. You can help with this, and even if none of it concerns your ancestors, you can be glad that you are working to index someone else's, while they are doing the same for yours.

Often, you can get in touch with others through the FHS; either actual cousins, who have seen your name and surname interests printed and write or phone, or people in your 'home' area with ancestors in yours, who are willing to swop work on small enquiries. This is very handy and here again, friendships are often forged.

INTERVIEWING ELDERLY RELATIVES

Ask the family

If you are collecting your family history, the first source must always be the family itself. You could, it is true, start knowing just your own name and date of birth, and work back through official records, but this is not only a very expensive way of going about things, but also a very chilly business, lacking the warmth and humour of family life, which turns clinical genealogy into living family history. Unless you are a complete orphan, you will be able to collect some of that precious personal knowledge for yourself.

When to start

Now. Even if you are too young to travel around gathering information from official repositories, or too tied to the house to spend much time on the work now, grab any possible opportunity. Talk to the older generation in the family and take careful note of what they have to tell you. Even if you can't make use of it now, store it up against the time when you have better chances to carry on the search. If you postpone starting until you have time, all the old folk may be dead and the rest not speaking to you because you never bothered with them before.

Who to ask

Anybody who is older than you (or anybody who has been in close contact with members of the family older than you). And don't be put off by those who say 'It's no use asking Aunt Fanny – she doesn't remember what she had for breakfast, poor dear'. That may well be true, but if your breakfast was boring plastic slop, you would want to forget it too. If you get her talking about the days when she was young and happy, you may find she has total recall of everything and everyone. Often, elderly people have ceased to communicate because no one will bother to communicate with them. Spend a little time with them and they will open up again. You may think that old people only talk about boring things like bingo and bowls. They think that young people only talk about boring things like pop records and football. True?

You will have to be prepared for a certain amount of problems at the beginning, and for some time being wasted on things you are not interested in or opinions you don't agree with. That applies to most television programmes, evenings out at the pub or dinner with the boss. It is up to you to steer the conversation round to more interesting channels – or listen with an open mind and maybe get interested.

Who to start on

Obviously, if Great-Aunt Fanny is over 90 and in frail health, you must approach her pretty soon. However, it is best, if you can, to practise your technique nearer home first, with Mum or sister Sally. Then if you get confused or start asking questions in a way that upsets them, you will know enough to do better when you see Auntie. It helps, too, if you have collected the more obvious stuff about the later generations of the family, and can start with some sort of pedigree in hand, rather than stopping Auntie every few minutes to spell or repeat a name. If you keep stumbling, or react with surprise to some well-known (to her) bit of family history, you are going to throw the old lady and maybe stop the flow. Cut your teeth on your nearest and dearest and try to get the background clear in your own mind. But if you hear that the end is nigh, don't fail to go on because you think you might make a mess of it. Better a mess than nothing at all. You might even give the old lady a new lease of life, because someone is interested at last.

Why not just write – or phone?

Distant relatives are best interviewed rather than written to, if this is at all practical. Why not go to Mudflat to see Auntie Maggie instead of joining the traffic jam to the coast next Bank Holiday? Some elderly people are not very good at reading or writing, either through lack of formal education or through failing sight or arthritic hands. Others just can't be bothered to put pen to paper, or don't see why they should, or write but forget to post the letter. In most cases, if only you went, you would get the answer you want. Even people who write are not usually as gloriously indiscreet on paper as they would be face to face. They won't commit to paper their opinion of Cousin Jane, in case she sees the letter, neither will they speculate about the parentage of Lizzie's baby – after all, you are a stranger and you might be shocked.

By all means write first to explain who you are and what you want, but try to follow it up with a personal visit if you possibly can. You could try phoning, but remember that some old people are rather scared of the phone, others don't talk freely into the air, never knowing who is listening, and many more are rather deaf and find it a strain to listen for long.

If you don't get an answer, this could be because of the mechanical problems when writing mentioned above; or because stamps cost money (and you forgot to include an SAE); or because that nice Mrs Brown offered to post the letter and forgot; or because they have lost the letter or forgotten it. After a decent interval, write again saying you are coming down next Wednesday and will call, but if it is not convenient, then how about Wednesday week, or would they suggest a day? This may get action, but if not, go on Wednesday – they can't say they haven't been warned. Don't just drop in – it embarrasses people to be caught in the middle of a mess, or without a biscuit in the house. An exception to that is if the old relative is a known recluse, given to locking the door and hiding. Then arrive (plus biscuits) and get your foot in the door – having made a noise like a milk bottle to get him to open up.

Prepare to meet thy doom

Time – set aside the whole day for the visit if necessary. You will get nowhere if you try to do the interview in a rush on the way to somewhere else. Don't keep looking at your watch – you have the rest of your life to play with – Auntie may only have a few months left.

Dress – carefully. If you go dripping mink, then you are a snob and would not possibly want to know the sordid truth about Uncle Charlie. Don't go to the other extreme and wear scruffy jeans – you are after the spoons, letting down the side, shaming her before the neighbours. Trousers at all on females upset some old folk. High fashion of any kind, especially on men, is worrying and punk hair-cuts irritate. You want something from Auntie, so make every concession to her suscepti- bilities. Nice, neat, conservative garments, no extremes of any kind. Park the Rolls where it will impress the neighbours but Auntie will only spot it after you have established yourself and been classed as a nice, friendly body, with no airs.

Children – not recommended under about twelve at all. The sweetest little angels turn into fiends when they are visiting. They resent not being the centre of attention, or, if they are, it distracts from the purpose of the visit. The cakes they stuff down them will return dramatically half way back up the motorway. Even sensible children behaving normally find problems in adapting their movements to a house not geared to the young. They knock over the Dresden shepherdess or break the handles off bone china or terrify the cat and budgie. If you must take the family, show them off all prettied up for five minutes, then send them off with a minder for the rest of the day (and a change of clothes). Let them back for the last fifteen minutes of the visit, mopped and subdued, then get rid of them before they start making remarks about uncle's red nose or the funny smell.

Photos of children are something else again. They may spark off an extra reminiscence about our Jimmie who used to look just like that before he was took.

Spouses and teenagers above the clodhoppy stage. They can be very useful, if they will sit tight and make the right noises. If they will look after the tape recorder (see page 27) or can take good photos, they are valuable indeed. But the sort of man who yatters on about his car and his importance and what he would say to the Unions if, or the woman who sits there like a Christian martyr, resenting every mention of the family, or the young horror who whines about being home in time for the disco are best left at home, or sent out as minders with the younger ones, or quietly pushed under a bus.

Dogs – preferably not. They are worse than children for knocking things down; they chase the cats; they dig up the flower bed; they bump into Auntie when she is carrying the tea tray. Even doggy households like their own dogs, not yours.

Cats – the native cat is sacred. Don't sit on her chair or brush her off your lap. Wear clothes which will stand being clawed or haired on and bite back the scream if you are bitten ('Tibby's got a bad ear, dear.').

Food – eat and drink whatever is put before you, with great enthusiasm but reasonable moderation. If you are actively allergic, say how much you love it but the wicked doctor has forbidden it. Otherwise, eat what comes and throw up later. You might even like it. If you are worried about the expense of the amount the family have eaten, then take along milk and bread (just happen to have it in the car) and some edible gift. If the amount provided is very considerable and obviously beyond their means, don't offer money. That is an insult. Send a replacement soon after – not precisely the same (ours isn't good enough) but similar (because you really know what good food is).

Smell – sometimes, old people's houses smell odd. Ventilation is a draught to them. Sometimes people smell odd. It isn't easy when you are frail and arthritic to keep yourself or your house spotless – besides, who ever comes round to see. So when you go in, don't sniff the air and ask for the windows to be opened. And don't stare round the room. You are there to talk, not to do a housing inspection. And, if the house is neat and clean, don't smoke cigarettes unless pressed. It takes weeks to get the stink out of covers and corners. Smoke can be actively distressing to someone with respiratory trouble.

Timing – old people may flag after talking for an hour or so (or they may go on until you are dropping in your tracks). If your interviewee shows the slightest sign of distress, let up for a while. She may recover after half an hour's nap, or that may be it for the day. So you are disappointed because you have come 85 miles. Auntie has come 85 years – how do you think she feels? You can surely come back again another day. Don't try to force more out of the old lady than she can give that day, or that will be the last chance you get to see her. Leave the house with the feeling that you can come back again and welcome (and don't wait too long).

Contacting distant relations

When you have exhausted the family you know well, there will come a stage when you start on those you haven't seen since you were six – or that your mother hasn't seen since *she* was six. After that come the interviews with complete strangers. Obviously, you will write first saying who you are and what you want. Tracing family history is acceptable as a form of madness nowadays, and establishing yourself as the family's genealogy nut is no bad thing.

Your motives must be made crystal clear. If the relative has money there will naturally be the suspicion that you are after it. If you discover that Aunt Maud is filthy rich, then do go in the mink bearing a single rose. What is more difficult is the more normal case where Auntie has a very little nest egg, which was valuable once. She is liable to think you are after the spoons, or, if you go on about how much money you have and how little you need her spoons, she will think you despise her treasures. Somehow, you have to spot an object which is attractive but by no means valuable and praise that. If you can convince Auntie that you rate the old tea caddy as highly as the spoons, then maybe you will get the lot one day. More important, you will get the story.

This is quite a difficult problem, for if you appear to scorn worldly goods, someone else will get what you covet as a memento of your ancestors. Somehow, you have to persuade the family that you are a suitable custodian for anything 'family', however trivial – or valuable, while getting it over that you are not 'after something' at the outset.

You will be going into someone else's house and asking them very personal questions. Can you persuade them that you are not a snooper from the Social Security in disguise? An elderly lady may not, anyway, like someone younger knowing all about her age and goings-on. You will have to persuade her that you are not just nosey – that you want to share her knowledge of the family and that you will understand her problems. This means establishing yourself, not as a great-great-niece, too young to be told all the naughty bits, but more as a sort of worldly-wise cousin, able to comprehend and enjoy all that is confided, without making moral judgements. It is quite possible to bridge the generation gap. People are people first, and age groups long after, so think yourself on to the same wavelength as your informant, and react as you would to a friend of your own age.

Cousin Flo. Very often, your aged person will be in the care of a middle-aged daughter or son. If you turn up on the doorstep, ready to charm the birds off the trees, you may meet a lot of resentment from the person who has to cope, day in, day out, with all the vagaries of which the elderly are capable. You have the time to be patient, the money to bring gifts, the stamina to pander for a couple of hours. Flo has got to cope with the reaction, the excitement, the demands for foie gras every day of the week and far more service than she is getting already. If this is the effect you have on Auntie, for sure she 'won't be well enough to see you' next time. Enlist Flo's help, flatter her, send her a little gift that she will really like, help with the washing up, understand her problems too. Try to leave a good impression on her, not just on Auntie. Remember that in the fullness of time, when Auntie is gathered to her makers, it is likely to be Flo who clears up those lovely family papers. She could burn them, or pass them on to you – which do you think will be likely?

You too can be an angel for a day at a time.

The sticky start

Sometimes, your relative won't play. The first stage is to identify yourself, if possible, by talking to her about someone she knows ('I'm your brother George's daughter Jean's daughter Carol') or showing photos of someone she knew at the date when she knew them. If you have that sort of photo, maybe get an enlarged print – old eyes find it difficult to see something half an inch high. If you have the family face yourself, then half the battle is won. Seize on any memory you, or your parents, have of visits to the relative long ago.

Sometimes relatives (old men especially) are coarse or rude, seeming intent on annoying you. Don't rise to it. It could be that they have not moved in polite circles for so long they have forgotten how. It could be that you are being tested to see if you are a squeamish townie, not fit to hear the truth about the family. Old people are entitled to be rude (about your weight, your nose, your lack of hair, the size of your family, the make of your car) and when you are ninety, you can take full advantage of this. It is all right for a female to answer back to a man, in a very teasing way, and for a male to tease Auntie, but don't cheek someone of the same sex.

Sometimes the interviewee just won't talk. Sometimes they have lost the habit of talking to people, sometimes because, perversely, now he has someone to talk to, Uncle wants to show his power by not doing so. Mothers who have potty-trained difficult infants can cope best with this line. Some people won't talk because they have something to hide, or because they think the family is too commonplace for you to want to hear about. You have to sell yourself as broad-minded but not immoral.

You know just how hard life was in the old days and how people didn't have the easy ways out they have now. This usually covers illegitimacy, desertion, drunkenness, thieving.

If false humility is the problem, make it clear you know Grandpa was a labourer and that you are interested in when he started work and who he worked for too. In fact, if the relative is just intent on being cagey about family facts, you can sometimes get him going by asking about the old days in general – compare farming then with now, ask him what it was like at school when he was a boy. If you really have to fight to get him talking, chatter on about your own family and bring each topic round to 'I bet you didn't go to school by bus' or 'Did you have a big birthday party when you were small' – hung on short statements about little Jason and young Emma. Use any universal topic to drag the conversation round by the scruff of its neck from now to then.

Don't get carried away and spent the whole of the time talking about yourself and your family, even if encouraged. You are not there to sell *your* importance, *your* brilliance, *your* wonderful children, *your* useless husband, but to listen and gather information. Once Uncle gets going, don't stop the flow to argue with his opinions. Does it matter if he is racist? – ask him who lived next door when he was a boy – he probably hated them too. If he talks football, don't blind him with science about modern teams – get him back to the first match he ever attended ('With his brother? Did his father go? What about his uncles? What were their names?')

If it is evident that Auntie is being cagey because of the presence of Cousin Flo, can you sell yourself as harmless enough to get Flo to go out for a nice walk (or a nice drive with your spouse) while you talk? The root of the trouble may be that Flo arrived too soon after the wedding, but mustn't be told, to protect her innocent spinsterhood, or her mother's moral superiority. Nods, becks and winks might convey that you have guessed, and get things flowing.

Smooth running

Once you have got the conversation going, by whatever means, the problem then is to keep it running smoothly, without jerks and stops. One of the most difficult things is being sure who Auntie is talking about at any one time.

It eases matters if you always refer to relatives in the terms in which she would think of them. Thus 'Father' is her father, 'Grandpa' her grandfather not yours. Establish quickly whether Grandpa is her father's father and Gramp her mother's, or vice-versa. Johnnie is your father, John your uncle on the other side. Bill is a brother and Willie a cousin. If you really can't work it out, ask once, then remember. Aim to keep the discussion to one generation at a time – this saves changing gear in mid-reminiscence from the 1940s to 1920s to Edwardian times.

However, don't ruin a promising train of chat because you haven't finished the list of Great-Uncle Ernest's dozen children. If you get the same story twice, either listen to see if new details come out or, if it can be managed discreetly, seize on something in the middle to use as a starting point for another story.

React to the stories as if they were new – a grievance of fifty years ago may still rankle and need sympathy. But don't treat the facts as quaint bygones, and don't judge past events by today's standards. There was not always access to contraception or hostels for battered wives, so don't tell Auntie she should have left the drunken brute early on, before the six children arrived.

Read up the background, of history (for dates) and social history. But don't get carried away by a passion for academic research. Don't get so excited by talking to a relic of the General Strike period that you demand an opinion on the socio-economic consequences of the Jarrow march – unless Uncle is an economic historian. But if you know a bit about the period under discussion, this stops your cries of wild surprise at the wages and prices. If you know what the norm was, you can concentrate much more on the reasons why one of your family varied from it. Learn some basic dates which can be used for reference (the two wars, the Strike, the Flu, the Abdication, etc).

If your informant has been chattering away nineteen to the dozen and suddenly clams up or goes cagey, think back to what you said. Did you mention Uncle Charlie – so what did he do to flutter the dovecote? Have you been pushing for dates of the marriage in front of Cousin Flo? If the latter, leave it – you can check at St Catherine's. If there is going to be no other source, probe gently, make a joke of wicked Uncle Charlie (a bit of a lad) but if Auntie looks distressed instead of mischievous, stop there. And never make a joke of her own mother or Granny.

Above all, don't push the elderly relative beyond his or her physical or mental endurance. Some frail bodies can't sit up for long, some frail minds can't stay clear for long. Watch out for signs of faltering and leave your questions there.

Recording

If you possibly can, record the interview. You won't remember the exact words said, and these may become important years later, after Auntie has passed to her reward. There is a difference between 'He was born in Richmond', 'He came from Richmond' and 'The family came from Richmond' (even before you start on *which* Richmond). If you try to write it all down, you will most likely fail, unless you are a proficient shorthand writer, and even then, all those hooks and squiggles are a bit daunting. What are you writing? Are you really from the Social Security after all? Why are you hunched over the book, not looking Auntie in the face? Besides, if you are copying, you are not comprehending and reacting to the information as it comes and asking the right questions about the discrepant bits.

If you can, take a tape recorder with you. If you know the person and the house, a reel-to-reel recorder will give you better quality – after all, this is likely to be a social document of some importance to the family, and potentially to some local or national historian. But if the person's reactions are doubtful, taking a tape recorder is a risk. Some may refuse to talk, some become stilted and edit out the naughty bits. Then, there is the little problem of plugs. There are some very odd bits of electric wiring in some elderly people's houses, and it doesn't help the flow of an interview if you have to change a plug from three-pin ring mains to those funny round things they use in Coventry.

If the reactions or mains equipment are at all doubtful, take a good battery cassette recorder. You may want to conceal the instrument, which is no problem as long as you have a good omni-directional mike close to the speaker – old voices don't carry far. You could mask the mike with your handbag or a camera or pretend it is an inhaler and snuffle a bit.

Provide the longest tape available, in case the going is good, and – ideally – have a quiet assistant to change tapes if necessary. Meanwhile, as you listen, take just a few notes of the rough layout of the family, so you can be totally clear if you need to ask questions, or to prompt the next round of reminiscence. This way, you can be an attentive audience while not losing a syllable. If you have to change the tape solo, then go to the loo and take the machine with you rather than stop Auntie in her tracks while you scrabble behind a chair.

Always label the cassette with the date and name, and remove it from the reach of any of the family with a habit of wiping old tapes for re-use.

Photos and pedigrees

Take with you as many photographs of the family as you can, even if you don't know quite who they are. Showing around mystery pictures is the best way to get them identified. Each relative you visit will probably have some photos. Just possibly, they might lend them, but more probably, they would let you make a copy on the spot. If you have a camera with a good portrait attachment (and ideally, someone to do it, who can concentrate on making a good job of it while you are talking) this will add to the value of your visit considerably. There is nothing like a photo to jog the memory. Even if the face is not recognised, the clothing may be – 'Our Jimmie had a sailor suit like that'!

Old photos have embossed stamps of the firm's name and address, if they are commercial ones (later ones have inked stamps on the back). The place may be worth asking about ('Why was cousin Marge in Heckmondwike?' 'For Jane's wedding to Herbert Oldroyd'.). Even landscapes and views of stately homes are not to be ignored. Did

Martha work at Dotheboys Hall? Is that the view from Uncle Fred's farm? Conventional postcards from resorts tell you which place the family went to for holidays. They may have messages on the back with family information too. Make a note of the non-portrait photos in the family album and use the information on them.

Take round a portfolio of family photos if you can. Always ask for identifications, even when you know, since this may start a reminiscence going. People don't necessarily always recognise photos of themselves, but they will of relatives. If you want to do the job properly, you can sepia-tone your modern copies of old photos – it looks more authentic and it's fun.

Whether you write out the whole family pedigree and show it to Auntie before you start is an arguable point. It will certainly help you to have a complete draft of all the information you know already. But will it impress Auntie, confuse her or make her feel redundant? If you know her well, you can judge. If not, perhaps make several pedigrees – one with complete information, in case you want to refer to it; one with year dates and only the direct line in detail; one very simple one showing your name and Auntie's and the link between the two. When you have judged which is suitable, produce it, and keep the others under wraps.

There is a big risk with producing a complete-looking pedigree. Even if Auntie has information which would correct some important error, she may not like to say – you've got it written down, it must be true, or she doesn't want to argue with a nice person like you. If any information is doubtful, leave it out, pencil it, and/or put a big question mark. Try to get a list of the family in order before showing her what Uncle Joe said. He could easily be wrong. By all means send her a copy of the pedigree afterwards, if she shows interest, but if she seems rather prim, do gloss over the awkward marriage to baptism dates, since she may show it to a nosey neighbour and be embarrassed by having the dread truth about Granny spread around the district.

What to ask them

You want names, dates, occupations, places first, then appearance, characters, habits, motives, odd sayings, etc. The first four you could at a pinch get from official sources, so if your interviewee is very frail, settle for the latter ones – which you will probably get nowhere else. But in normal circumstances, if you have worked back through the family, up the generations, you should be able to collect enough basic information to save you pounds on certificates.

Ask the informant about his or her own family – the brothers and sisters, in order of birth, their full names (since pet names sometimes bear no relation to the registered name), their lives as young persons. If a great deal of detail on one brother, including his marriage and current address, emerges, go along with this, but if you are able to prompt, keep the informant's mind on one time period – more detail will come out that way. Ask where the children went to school, what clothes they wore, what jobs around the house they did, whether one was the favourite (jealousy fifty years on is a powerful spur to memory). When you have exhausted the children, ask about the father and mother, then their brothers and sisters, then the grandparents. Try to get it clear which side of the family you are talking about, referring to each person in the terms in which they would be known to your informant (Aunt Mary's boy Joe is *her* Aunt Mary, not yours). Don't be surprised if an elderly person doesn't know the first name of his grandparents – children were not encouraged to be familiar. You may be lucky if you get the surname of the mother's father. And be wary – Grandpa Sutton may be the grandfather who lived in Sutton, though his name was Foljambe.

Getting dates is more awkward. Unless your family is uncommonly numerate, then remembering actual dates is a difficult business. If you ask Auntie for the year when her brother Jim was born, she will either fret about not remembering, spend hours trying or pull some arbitrary date out of the air to shut you up. Ask for date order instead – was Jim older, how many years older, was he at school when Mary was born, and so on. If you can get this sort of comparison between the previous family members mentioned, and then get one fix on the date of one of them, you can work out the rest.

Use national, local or personal events as fixed points for dating the family. Establish whether something happened 'before the War' (which war?), 'after the Somme', 'in Coronation Year' (whose?); the year Arsenal won the Cup or Midnight Sun won the Derby; just before they built the Cottage Hospital; when they had the pageant at the Hall; the year I left school, got married, had our Georgie; buried Fred. The more cross-checks you get the better, then any mistakes will be cancelled out.

Most people remember the day and month of their own birthdays and those of their siblings and parents. The year may be hazier. Sometimes people can do age (even of long-dead people had they lived until now) but not the simple sums which provide the years. Obviously, you must not accept everything you are told as correct, but if the date given matches the official entry in the indexes at St Catherine's House, then it is probably right. If the year is wrong, perhaps the day and month are correct, and you will find the entry in the corresponding quarter for the year before or after. Death dates are more likely to be wrong than births or marriages. Try to get a double fix on these – both 'before the last war' and 'while I was still at school'. (People do remember the age and even the day when they left school, especially if they were poor scholars.)

You can check all national events in books and newspapers, and local ones in the latter source or a local history book. Don't stop the flow of the narrative to get out your little notebook and verify the date on the spot. It obviously helps if you carry at least some dates in your head – the two Wars for a start – so that you can tell if there is some major discrepancy between 'Grandpa died in the Flu,' (ie 1919) and 'I was only a baby then' when she must have been at least 14 by 1919 by other evidence.

Locations. Some people can recall a whole lot of addresses where the family once lived, some have only vague notions of the town or even the house (red brick, on the corner). Anything may help which gives a notion of where the family lived at a certain date or 'always till a while ago'. The place where a non-motoring family went for holidays may be significant. Sometimes people went to relatives, or to their vicinity. For a southern-based family to holiday at Scarborough or Skegness or Yarmouth a link with the north is likely. (But Yarmouth may not be Great Yarmouth, but the one on the Isle of Wight ('The Island'). And 'The Island' is Man to a Lancastrian and Canvey to an East Londoner.)

Occupations. Most people know what their fathers and siblings did. What Grandfather did may be known if they lived in the same place or holidayed with him. Watch out for 'enhancement'. If you look the sort who scorns common ancestors, then the farm labourer will become a farmer, a clerk a merchant, which could waste a lot of your time looking for him in directories where he won't appear. If she says farmer, ask how many acres (*not* hectares)/horses/labourers, etc – and drop the inquisition if she gets shifty.

What was he like? This is the most valuable sort of detail a really elderly person can give you. Some people will give you a physical description, some a character study (or assassination). You rarely get both, so don't worrit a person who sees beneath the surface for un-memorable things like colour of hair and eyes.

Who dun it? Victorians and Edwardians were so good at cover-ups that the identity of the 'real father' of a child is often shrouded in mystery. Auntie may be the only one to know, so you will have to ask her. But get on good terms first, display your unshockability and desire for the truth. Women generally know the truth rather than men – and will often only tell another woman – men have to be protected from harsh reality.

Tracing long-lost cousins

When you run out of all possible family sources, try the stranger who might belong. Finding him may involve a bit of detective work (so does genealogy).

If you have an uncommon surname, go through phone books for the British Isles (at the reference library) or even for the world (large reference libraries or the Guildhall Business Library or very large Post Offices. Extract all the addresses of the Bloggses or Fitzfazackerleys and get writing, or phoning if no result. You should receive a fair proportion of replies. The less common the name, the more interest in fellow sufferers. Don't forget to give information about yourself, if you expect to receive it from others.

Check if the name is already registered as a 'One Name Study', and if so, write to the named researcher, who may put you in touch with what sounds like your own kin. If there is no group, consider forming one. Information on how to organise One Name Studies is obtainable from the Guild at the address listed.

Even if your name is more popular, you can try the same thing just in the ancestral area. If it is very common, start with people listed who have family names or initials, or who are closest to the ancestral village, or in the same or a similar trade. If none of the right surname are listed, then write to the local paper, as mentioned above, detailing what you know of the family in that area. This may reach married ladies or people of your surname with no phones or ex-directory numbers. Don't forget to thank the Editor later for printing your letter and mention any contacts – which gives you an extra run of publicity for your name.

The weekend safari

A visit to the area on a weekday will allow you to search the electoral registers at the Post Office (or library) for those of your surname. Tell the counter assistant what you are doing. She may have heard people discussing the letter and know someone who meant to write but our Jack lit the fire with the paper dear. A passing postman could direct you to the house of a married daughter. Mention your interest at the library and the local shops – they may have suggestions of people to contact, including the lady who cared for old Mr Bloggs (and heard all his reminiscences sixty times over) and still writes to the family.

Even a Sunday visit can be turned to good account. Some shops are open. Drop into the local pub and ask some of the oldest inhabitants if they remember the Bloggs family. It will involve you in buying a few pints (say *'have a beer'*, not *'have a drink'*, which translates as double whiskies all round), but it could get you details (possibly scurrilous) of Grandpa's mis-spent youth or prowess at football.

Females are usually better value for names, dates, and where they are now, but approaching old ladies may be best done through an intermediary, especially if there have been con-men round the place lately. Some may go to church (so could you, and sit in the same pews where your ancestors sat) and if you introduce yourself to the vicar or verger, they may introduce you to a likely long-term resident. If you are given names of possible informants, say 'Mrs Brown said you might be able to help'. They are more likely to know the married name of Jenny Bloggs who was at school with them, and that she is visiting her married daughter in Birch Close today.

Never be shy about contacting possible unknown relatives . . . if you are very polite, cheerfully prepared to go away and come back later, when they have had a chance to clean up a bit. Don't expect strangers to roll out the red carpet on sight, though. Don't call at lunch time, or at night on elderly ladies living alone. Don't expect to be recognised and welcomed immediately. People tend to reject unknown cousins as 'not belonging to us'. Take the family photos, especially those connected with the place, which give you credentials.

Down among the dead men

Go down to the churchyard too and see if there are any family tombstones still there. These may give birth as well as death dates and some family members are brought back from distant places for burial, or people dying abroad may be commemorated on a stone. Sometimes the older stones have been moved or broken up, and if so, there should have been details recorded at the time. There ought to be a copy in the parish, so ask the vicar or verger about this. If the sexton is around, he may have burial books, or just know where families are buried. Don't ignore people of a different name buried in the middle of a group of 'family' stones. They could be married daughters.

Many town churchyards were closed for burial in the 1850s, and you will have to visit the local cemetery. They may have burial books on the premises (in the Superintendent's lodge) or may be able to tell you where they are. These give name, age, address and the details of the person arranging the burial. The other people buried in a purchased tomb will be kin, though poor folk were buried in common graves with strangers.

People have short memories. If your ancestors left more than 75 or 80 years ago, be prepared for a flat statement that they were never there at all. Even when you are sure there is a connection, some folk will say they never had a great-uncle Herbert at all. Be polite, leave your name and address, and maybe memory will work better later on.

'She died last week'

All too often, you track down an elderly relative, only to find that death has just beaten you to it. Tact demands that you stay away from a house of mourning. The call of family history demands that you get in there fast before all the papers are burnt. But be very, very tactful, or the bereaved will think you are after the spoons. Handled carefully, you may be a valuable source of comfort for a lonely person picking up the threads after years of caring for an invalid. You may even come away with a mass of 'useless rubbish' which is pure genealogical gold. Mind that you do not upset the executor, who is custodian of all the effects.

If the old person lived alone, you may trace the next of kin through newspaper reports of the funeral, or addresses on the floral tributes on the grave. Neighbours may be able to tell you the addresses. Indeed, if the neighbours were confidantes, they may be able to tell you all about the family and know as much about your ancestors as you do. Other places to find friends of the deceased may be at the Darby and Joan Club, the W.I., the Labour or Conservative Club, the British Legion, the Bingo Club, the local pub, even the church or chapel. This copes with most of the gossiping places of the able-bodied – except the local shop.

House-bound or bedridden people may have been visited by the W.V.S. lady, a home-help, a Guide or Scout or school youth club member who regularly ran errands; a hairdresser or chiropodist, the pools collector, the milkman, someone from the church, old Harry down the road or – above all – a social worker. If any of them listened to stories of the past, they may be able to repeat them for you. Social workers may have collected information about the family in an effort to contact relatives. If you appear to be the only next of kin, they may talk to you and reveal what they know. But they can turn very officious, especially if you happen to be a journalist – they are sensitive about being investigated, and may feel they could have handled the case better, had there been time.

The last person in charge of an elderly invalid often knows a great deal about the family – which is why daughters-in-law are often better informants than sons, out at work all day. Often grandchildren will be told more than children – there is no need to keep up a front for them. Some grandfathers are awful liars, though, and lead children astray.

Family traditions

Every family has its traditions and, inevitably, they are not all true. They are not false either. Don't believe every word Auntie says because she looks so innocent. Maybe she is quoting Uncle Bert, who thinks he is Napoleon. Work out whether your informant was there, was adult and still remembers things. If not, what was her source? It may be Auntie Flo who was addicted to romantic novels, the aforesaid Uncle Bert, or a remark she overheard when she was four.

The tradition most likely to be true is the one that offers no advantage to the family. 'Grandpa came from Wiltshire' – yes, sounds reasonable. 'Grandpa was the cousin of the Earl of Mucke' – well, treat with caution. Some traditions can be proved true as soon as the official documents are checked. These are simple.

Some are true, but in a different century – great-grandpa came from Wiltshire, the five times great-grandpa was cousin to Sir Henry Mucke. Some traditions are true but misunderstood. 'The family used to live at Ashby Castle' = they used to live at Ashby de la Zouche (alias Castle Ashby). A child may overhear that Grandpa had 'connections' with the Duke of this or the Earl of that. True. But this may turn out to be as landlord (or potman) of a pub of that name or arms. Keeping the Pig (and Whistle) becomes 'hog ranching' to an emigrant grandchild.

Some traditions are misremembered. My grandmother, a lady of impeccable veracity, said her mother's maiden name was Bowman. I finally found her as Moorman. Granny said triumphantly 'I knew it was something to do with a boat'.

Some things were told to your informant as the truth and retailed as such. In this class come most of the stories that Great-granny was seduced by the local Squire, never the butcher, the baker or a passing tinker. Check for probability. If she was plain and 36 and the Squire had a string of glamorous mistresses, probably not. If she was young, very pretty, worked at the manor and the local paper says he was at home at the relevant time, well, maybe. If the child in question is the image of the ffoulenough ancestors, rather than of the bootboy she married three months later, well, even more maybe. If she was given a huge dowry and the child was later educated beyond his station, well, very likely indeed. Don't believe everything you are told – but don't ignore it either.

The documents in the case

Every family has about its collective person some useful documents. Apart from birth, marriage and death certificates, wills, and insurance policies, which you may be allowed to see and copy details from, there are other things to ask for. Memorial cards and funeral certificates; grave-space receipts; Granny's birthday book, with all the family names in it; school and Sunday school reports and prizes; apprenticeship indentures; army Rolls of Honour (death date, rank and regiment); samplers (name, age and date); birthday present books, photos (mentioned earlier); sports and hobby trophies; holiday souvenirs (a Present from Clacton); army or navy mementoes (regiment, ship?); souvenirs of the British Raj (who served in India?) and receipts, which are kept for an incredible time and give addresses and some idea of lifestyle. And there might even be a family bible.

You should never turn down anything as trivial or useless. Gain a family reputation as a home for any old rubbish – and one day it will pay off.

The written questionnaire

If you must write, because you are tied to the house or the relative is overseas, you will have to explain what you are after and give information about yourself and your immediate forebears. Then you have a choice. You can say vaguely, 'Tell me all about your family', or send a questionnaire with very detailed requests and a space for the answer to be filled in. The first risks getting 'I am a widow and have no family left over here'. The second risks being thrown in the bin as impertinent nosiness. Possibly a combination of both is the best you can do. Some people will junk the form and write a letter, some will fill in some of the form, some, bless them, will do both. Some won't answer at all. But usually people overseas are keener to know of links with home than people who live in Britain.

A sample for one person is:

Your father's name ....

His date of birth .... Where born ....

His school(s) .... (dates)

His career (jobs in order) .... (2–3 lines)

Was he in the army/navy/airforce ....

Regiment, ship, squadron ....

Where did he serve ....

Where did he live .... (please give dates)

.... (3–4 lines)

Date of death .... Where ....

Where buried ....

Date of marriage .... Where ....

(similar details of your mother)
(list and dates of children).

Repeat this for everyone you think might be known – stating very clearly 'your father's father', 'your mother's father' not 'grandfather'.

If you want information about all the brothers and sisters and their families, you will have to provide a lot of sheets of paper, and this is going to cost rather a lot to post. Sent airmail overseas you will reach 50p in no time – so select carefully before you commit yourself to writing to every single person of the name. It is polite to send an SAE inland or two International reply coupons (from the Post Office) overseas. It will soon mount up, so unless you pick and choose, it is going to cost a fair bit. Moreover, these IRCs are very poor value, costing about 40p+ each and exchanging at about 20p, and everyone writing abroad gripes about them. You could try sending English stamps, explaining what you are doing. They can't be used in reply, but can be sent to UK correspondents by people over there, which saves *them* paying 50p+ for IRCs.

If you join a Family History Society here, your surname interests will circulate to FHSs abroad and you could send a general appeal to them to ask their own members. That way, you would be tapping interested people directly.

Remember

It isn't necessarily true because Auntie Maggie said it.
It isn't necessarily a lie because Uncle Bert said it.
If none of the names check at St Catherine's, try a different year. If there is still no sign, are you looking for pet names?
Polly (or Molly) is Mary Anne (or Mary).
Sally or (rarely) Sadie is Sarah.
Tillie or Mattie is Matilda.
Nellie is Ellen or Eleanor or Helen.
Patty (or Matty) is Martha, not Patricia till 1920 plus.
Peggy or Meg or Maggie or Molly is Margaret – so is Greta sometimes.
Jenny or Jinny is Jane or Jean or Joan or Janet.
Fred is Frederick or Alfred.
Bert is Albert or Herbert or Robert – Bertie is Bertram.
Lal is Lawrence or Albert; Loll, Lowry, Larry is Lawrence.
Bessie, Lizzie, Libby, Betty, Beth, Liza is Elizabeth (or Eliza).
Nora might be Eleanora, Honora.
Nancy is Ann.
Dolly is Dorothy – so is Dora, sometimes.
Cissie might be Cicely but is usually = Sister, so could be anything.
Nip(per), Kid(da) – general term for younger brother.
Biddy – (Bridget) but general term for old woman.
Bessie – (Elizabeth) but general term for interfering old woman.

The next step

Everything you discover will need to be checked with official records. The most important are the basic entries of birth, marriage and death, held at the General Register Office or 'St Catherine's House' in London. First, go through what you have collected from the family and make a rough family tree or even a list of the family names in order, with date deductions.

Aunt Fanny says she was 77 in May 1989 and her birthday is on July 10. So she was born in July 1911.

Her brother Jack was four years older 'to the day' so he should be born in July 1907. Maggie and May were the oldest of the lot, Jimmy would have been 76 next week but he died in the Flu. (So May 1913–1919.) Drew wanted to join the army – but he was just turned thirteen on Armistice Day (11 November 1918 so born October/November 1905), Georgie was born while Father was away putting the cisterns in the hospital for the soldiers back from the Somme (1916); Edie was the baby.

Uncle Harry always lived in Heatherby and died there just after VE day. He'd been retired a good long time (his tombstone in the churchyard of Handley says he was 75 and died in 1946 (just after VJ Day).

That means he was born in 1871, which is a census year – a valuable date, you will find. When you check up, you find his death registered in Birmingham, because he died in hospital there. Aunt Fanny was away visiting her sister Edith who'd just had a baby and complications, so she missed the fun and the funeral.

Grandfather Bloggs lived with us in his last years. He was buried in the churchyard a bit before the war. (The broken tombstone says *James A . . . Bloggs aged 81 died 20 J . . . 1931*, but the wife's name has gone.)

Uncle Barty 'spoke with a funny accent' and died not long after the Coronation. (When you check, it isn't 1951, the coronation of Elizabeth II, but 1937, that of her father, George VI. Bartholomew died in late 1937, aged 55, it says, but the only Bartholomew Jardine was born in late 1880 in Newcastle on Tyne district, so someone wasn't sure of his age.)

So you have a list of precise dates to check, and the approximate ones for Margaret and May. Margaret is there all right in the first quarter of 1902, but no May, at least under that name. A lot of Mays were Mary, like 'Princess May of Teck', wife of George V. This one turns out to have been named Victoria (because she was born on May 24, the old Queen's birthday and was known as 'our May flower').

The date of birth for Margaret will give a further lead to the date of the marriage between Andrew Bloggs and Alice Jardine, which could be the first certificate you necessarily buy, since it will take you into the next generation, about whom you know nothing much at all.

Getting a birth certificate for Harry Bloggs will give you an address for the family in 1871, which is important (see the chapter on Censuses); getting one for Bartholomew would give you the location for the Jardine family in 1880, near enough to a census date.

However, not everyone will have a useful list from the family, and some people will be stuck with just one lead. If father was George Smith instead of George Bloggs, and all that was known about him was that he lived at one time in a large city, tracking him down could be tough. You couldn't write to all the Smiths in Sheffield with any hope of information. You would have to start by getting his birth certificate – given an exact date – and even then, there could be a dozen possible entries in the indexes. If so, you would have to get his marriage certificate, which states a father's name. Even then, it would be slow going, so the only hopeful lead might be your mother's name.

If getting to London is difficult or a day free from responsibilities is a matter for great contrivance, it may hardly be worth going up just to order one certificate. As you will gather, you can't actually see more than the indexes on the first visit, and only when you have a certificate in your possession (after a minimum two full days) can you go further.

Postal applications to St Catherine's for certificates are not practical. If you are totally sure of the place and year, the local registrar covering that area can supply a certificate by post for the basic £5.50 fee. If – as is more usual – you aren't sure of the place, then it may be simpler to have someone else order that first certificate – perhaps a friend, or someone contacted through the FHS. Several of them have a 'courier service' whereby a London member will order and collect certificates, and even make short searches, for a small fee over the basic. These couriers are heavily used and work in their lunch hours as volunteers, so the wait could be considerable.

If the facts are in doubt, and the search is likely to be complicated, then it is fairer to use a professional searcher. The certificate costs £5.50 – the inclusive service will total £8.50 to £10 (depending on search time), if you use one of the individual searchers who advertise. Large firms charge VAT as well.

If access to London is easy and your time is less constricted, it is a good idea to go up and get familiar with St Catherine's and maybe the other repositories in an unhurried way, but if you need to make every minute count, take a few short cuts.

There are some provincial locations (page 56) where at least some of the St Catherine's indexes can be seen in public libraries or Record offices. Mormon libraries (page 58) can order the films for you for a small fee apiece. A few retain these indexes permanently.

ST CATHERINE'S HOUSE:
The General Register Office

Certificates and indexes

All records of births, marriages and deaths registered in England and Wales since 1 July 1837 are available to public access. They are in the custody of the Office of Population, Censuses and Surveys, St Catherine's House, 10 Kingsway, London WC2B 6JP (present home of the Registrar General). At present, you cannot see the actual entry, only the indexes of events. When you have found the right entry in the index, you have to buy an actual certificate to get further information. Each certificate costs £6, applied for in person. If you send for it by post, they charge a staggering £12 plus *even if you have the complete reference from their indexes*, and £15 plus if you only know the year, so the fewer you buy, the better. Collect every scrap of information from the family first, about names, dates, ages, where the family lived, *then* start certificate buying.

There are separate indexes for births, marriages and deaths, all filed in date order. Each year is divided into quarters. All events registered between 1 April and 30 June 1920 (say) are in JUN 1920, and all events registered from 1 July to 30 September are in SEPT 1920. Remember that births, in particular, may be registered some weeks after they occur, so JUN 1920 will include children born in March and even some in February, and MAR 1920 may have children born late 1919. In each quarter, surnames are in alphabetical order, exactly as they are spelt, and this may not be the way you think they should be spelt. For each surname, entries are then in order of Christian name, also alphabetically.

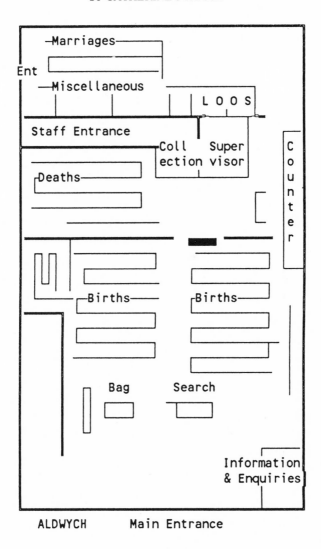

The indexes do not give the exact place where a person was born, etc, only the name of the Superintendent Registrar's District. This could be the same as a medium-sized town, or part of a city like London, or the nearest market town to a village. It helps to have a look at the map beforehand, or you can check up in the location books at the front desk at St Catherine's, which tell you the Superintendent Registrar's district for each small place.

WARNING. The index books are heavy and large, especially the older, handwritten ones, and you need strength to lift them around. Don't try it if you are old or in frail health, but enlist a sturdy young relative. The older books are dirty, too, so don't wear your best or light clothes – in colour, that is. You will get hot, so strip down to something thin and loose. It gets busy after 11 a.m., so go early.

There are currently proposals to restrict access to indexes less than 75 years old to close relatives, and to make earlier indexes available on microfilm, with some form of direct access to the actual registers of certificates, either by personal copying or through photostats. This will be in general terms similar to the Scottish system (see page 49). BUT the proposed fees are suggested as more than double, up to £20 a day. Nothing has yet been decided about this and the implementation of the proposals may be well in the future. Watch the press for further comments.

Getting started

You can start at any point for which you have accurate information, working back all the time from what you know to what you don't know. For the sake of those with little to go on, I have assumed for the moment that all you know is your own and your mother's date of birth. If you are looking for, say, Ruby Jane Crompton, born in February 1919, locate the year 1919 from the dates written on the end of the green open shelves in the first section, then the MAR 1919 index with the letter 'C' on it. Under 'Crompton' you will find something like this (all references invented):

Surname of parent	Name(s) or sex of child	Maiden surname of mother	Supt. Reg. Dist.	Vol.	Page
CROMPTON	Robert	BROWN	Worcester	5c	111
CROMPTON	Ruby Jane	HARRIS	Hackney	2c	222
CROMPTON	Ruth Mary	GREEN	Lewes	3d	333

(This applies to all births registered from Sep 1911 onwards.)

Copy down the complete details for Ruby Jane, including the year and quarter, check for accuracy, then go up the steps and fill in an application form. Take it to the Post Office-type counter and pay over your £5.50. The choice is of collecting the certificate in person (or via a friend armed with the receipt) or having it sent by post, free second class, or, if you provide a stamp, first-class. Both collection and first class post will take four days, second class post a week plus. This applies to straightforward cases, where all details on the form are correct.

Application directly by post should be made to OPCS, Smedley's Hydro, Southport, Lancs, remembering to enclose the higher fee of £12 with full reference or £15 without, but with precise details for identifying the event. Reference check (q.v.) case take longer, and postal applications without close details may be returned. On the whole, if you are uncertain, make a personal search (there may be index copies near you) or employ a London record agent (several advertise in 'Family Tree Magazine').

Any applications where the information on the form does not tally with that in the registers are returned negative, minus a checking fee. This usually happens where a figure has been miscopied or is unclear, or the wrong year and quarter are stated.

Don't add a second name, alter the name order or spelling, even if the person later used a different version from that recorded in the index. If your version doesn't tally with the index or original register version, they will reject the application, so forget that Mum signed her name Rubella Janina after she moved to Brighton.

The **birth certificate** will tell you the name of both parents, and from this you can get their **marriage certificate**, starting with the quarter when the baby was born and working back systematically, making sure you don't miss an index book. After MAR 1912 you will see (in the Marriage indexes:

Surname	Christian name(s)	Surname of spouse	Supt. Reg. District.	Vol.	Page
CROMPTON	Matthew James	HARRIS	Islington	1b	123

In the same quarter year under Harris, you will find:

HARRIS	Ada Jane	CROMPTON	Islington	1b	123

Copy down the year, quarter and reference carefully and get *that* certificate too. It will show the ages of the couple, which leads you to *their* birth certificates, and so on.

Before SEPT 1911 for births and MAR 1912 for marriages, the maiden name of the mother and the name of the spouse are not shown. The entries look like this:

SEP 1890	CROMPTON Henry Charles	St Pancras	1b	456

Unless you know from the family or the birth index of a younger sibling of Matthew born after 1911, you will have to wait for his birth certificate to get his mother's name – Louisa Batt. Then check the same quarter and find:

BATT Louisa	St Pancras 1b 455 – *wrong*
BATT Louisa Maud	St Pancras 1b 456 – *right*

because the reference must check exactly, one figure out won't do. People often drop or add names.

If you have the name of the husband, and it is uncommon enough, you could try getting a certificate after finding his reference alone, without the wife's name. This is a bit of a risk, since even the oddest combination of names may be given to two or three cousins all named after Grandpa. If you check for alternatives and find none at all, it is worth doing, to save time. You will have to check it out as soon as possible, but even a wrong branch of the same family may be useful. You couldn't do this with a common combination of names, because it could be a different family entirely, and waste time and money – so do all the steps in the right order.

'Double barelled' names, especially with '-Brown', '-Smith', '-Jones', etc, will normally be found under the second surname.

Multiple choice

As you go back, double Christian names will get less common and the more likely you are to be faced by a number of 'possibles'. For instance (births):

1. HARRIS James	Plymouth	5b 231
2. HARRIS James	Hackney	1b 342
3. HARRIS James	Rochdale	8b 435
4. HARRIS James	Colne	8b 534
5. HARRIS James	Birmingham	6d 654
6. HARRIS James	Birmingham	6d 987

Here the knowledge you have built up may help you. If all the events so far have been in East London, then probably '2' is your man. If he is likely to be West Country, or father was a sailor, then '1'. If you are pretty sure he came from Lancashire, then either '3' or '4'. You might be able to eliminate one if you look at the indexes of deaths, starting in the same quarter year. So many children died as infants that you might find:

HARRIS James   0   Colne   8b 23 (0 = birth to 1 year)

The ages at death are given from JUN 1866. They are often guesswork for older people, but right for babies. In this case, very likely the Rochdale one is yours.

This would not help if your ancestor came from Birmingham, even if one died there. You will have to use the Reference Checking system.

Reference Checking

There is a leaflet about this available at St Catherine's, but, basically, you will have the name of his father from his marriage certificate, say, as William. Tell the official you wish to do a reference check, and he will give you a form. Enter the two (or more) references on it and on the back write

'Father's name – William Harris'.

This is your Checking Point. Don't go mad and include the occupation, which has probably changed in twenty-odd years. You can tell them to 'stop at first entry' which matches the Check Point or have them do the lot. In the first case, they refund the fees for any entries not checked. In the second, there might be two 'correct' ones and you would have to pay for two certificates. The danger in 'stopping at first found', with a common name, is that there may be listed first *a* James Harris with a father named William, but he isn't yours. If you had all the potential choices at one go, you could probably tell which was right. It works out cheaper than going back later for a re-check, or getting the certificates one by one. And you won't be led into following up the wrong line of family.

'Full age' or minor

On many marriage certificates before 1870 or so, the couple are said to be of 'full age'. This means 21 or more, perhaps a lot more. Start looking for the birth at marriage year minus 21 and work back. If the age is given as 'minor', this is under 21. In the case of girls, it is probably not less than 15, or for boys, less than 17, though lesser ages are theoretically possible. Unless the problem can be solved fairly quickly, a check from the age at death (which may be a guess) or evidence from the censuses, especially 1851 to 1891, is likely to be necessary.

Birth certificates . . .

show:

The Superintendent Registrar's district and sub-district;
The place of birth – the street in a town, but probably only the village name in the country;
The exact day, month or year;
The time of day for twins, and occasionally for other children;
The name of the father and his occupation;
The forename of the mother, her married name, followed by 'formerly' and her maiden name;
The date of registration;
The name and address of the informant and whether he/she could write or not;
The name of the registrar;
Any name given at baptism and entered after being reported to the registrar.

A woman who has been married before should have her current married names; 'late', her previous married name; and 'formerly', her maiden name, or 'formerly [maiden name] but late [first married name]'. However, if the registrar did not know, or ask the right questions, this information is not always stated in every birth entry for the second family.

A bastard child has a blank for the father's name, with the name and occupation of the mother only stated. Only if the illegitimate father accompanied the mother (or sent an affidavit from overseas) could his name be given to the child and entered in the 'father' column. In this case, the mother's name will appear as 'Mary Jones' (or whatever her maiden name is) only, instead of 'Mary Brown formerly Jones'.

Marriage certificates . . .

show:

Name and district and church/chapel/register office;
Full date of marriage;
Name of groom;
His age (full = 21 or over), bachelor, widower or divorcee;
His occupation;
His residence (not always full street address);
His father's name and occupation;
The bride's name;
Her age (or 'minor' = under 21), spinster, widow or divorcee;
Sometimes an occupation;
Residence;
The name and occupation of her father;
Whether the marriage was by banns or licence;
Denomination of the church;
Whether the couple signed or made a mark to their names;
Names and signatures or marks of the witnesses;
Name of the clergymen or registrar.

The signatures are not the originals, but a copy made for sending in to the Register General. They should copy spelling exactly – if they can read it.

Before 1890, weddings in chapels had to be attended by the Registrar as well, to make sure the proper formalities were observed. After 1890, the pastor could be designated as an 'authorised person', and check up on himself.

Often the same address is given for both parties in a town. This does not necessarily mean they were both normally living together or even there. Giving the same address avoided paying for two sets of banns in different parishes. 'Residence' was established by putting a suitcase in the bride's house for three weeks.

Death certificates

show:

District and sub-district;
Place of death – full address or village name;

Name and sex of deceased;

Age, which may be guesswork for old people;

Occupation, for men or single women; or name and occupation of the husband of a married woman (sometimes of a widow) and the father for a child;

Cause of death;

Nature and duration of contributing illnesses;

Possibly medical attendant's name;

Date when registered;

Name and address of the informant, who should be a relative or person present at the death;

Registrar's name;

Corrections or additional details.

Burial could not take place without a death certificate, so registration was rapid in normal circumstances. In the case of violent or accidental death, an inquest was held and the Coroner is the 'informant'.

Free information

The indexes show:

Age at death from JUN 1866;

Mother's maiden name in births from SEP 1911;

Spouse's surname in marriages from MAR 1912;

Date of birth in deaths from 1969 – but this may be an estimate.

The extra information given in the very latest type of certificate will be useful in the future, but is less likely to concern present-day family historians, since it is closer to living family information and probably freely available at home.

The indexes are not infallible, either as copies of what is contained in the main registers, or as records of events as they occurred. Bad writing or inattention may have caused a misreading at any stage.

Other free information can be collected or deduced. List all entries of uncommon surnames (one which occurs only once or twice a quarter). List all entries, even of commoner surnames, in one registration district, one county, one geographical area. (You can pick out even unfamiliar places where the volume number matches the one which you know is your territory – all the '5c' entries, or all the '8d's.) Sort what you have collected into family groups – they often tie in with names the family have given you, or will jog people's memories.

If there is an uncommon Christian name in your family, note all references to it, even if in the 'wrong' part of the country. It could be where your family originally came from.

Pick one entry from a 'family group' from a census year (1841, 1851, 1861, 1871, 1881, 1891) and get that certificate. It will cost you £5.50, but key you in to further free information, which you might not get from the certificate for your direct ancestor born halfway between those years.

Local Register Offices

These serve a small area only, and the boundaries may have changed from what they covered a century ago. The offices are not geared to having people come in to make a general search; you can do this for a daily fee, but strictly by appointment. On the whole, use copies of St Catherine's indexes for major searches, then apply to the local office.

If you know the exact place and the date within a year or two; if you know the exact date and the place within a parish or two; if you are faced with a multiple choice at St Catherine's, and have good identifying material (like the Christian names of both parents and an unusual trade or something else you wouldn't risk using as a check point at St Catherine's, where they are very literal), you may be able to get a certificate locally for the basic fee, even by post or on the spot.

There are no consolidated indexes in local offices (but see the section listing locally-held microfilms), and events stay in the form in which they are submitted. Marriages are filed in a separate book for each church or chapel, and this book is only handed in when full. If the church is still using a book which was issued in 1850, then there is no local copy of that marriage at all held by the registrar. The duplicate was passed straight on to the General Register Office that quarter. Births and deaths are filed by sub-district.

The staff will make limited searches for entries where enough information is given to them to do so. If you lack enough identifying information as above, search copies of St Catherine's indexes first, and make a likely guess. Then send the local office the year and quarter, not the rest of the St Catherine's reference data – it doesn't mean a thing locally. But if you have good data, and just want a certificate for one missing piece, then the local office is quicker, more helpful and a lot cheaper by post, since they don't charge twice as much for nothing.

Scotland

Registration started on 1 January 1855 and all records are held at the General Register Office, New Register House, Edinburgh EH1 3YT (in West Register Street, off Princes Street, opposite the North British Hotel). The certificates cost £10 by post including a search covering 5 years, if you have reasonable identifying information. You can imagine that 'James Stewart, born somewhere in Scotland, somewhere between 1860 and 1870' would have too many possible entries, but 'James Stewart, son of Robert, a tailor, born approximately 1866–68' might do. If they can't find it – and they are very thorough – they deduct £2.00 odd for the work and refund the rest.

You can go there in person and for a daily fee of £9 odd have access not only to the indexes but the actual registers of events, from which you can copy down all the information, or, if you wish, buy a half price certificate as a souvenir on that day. There are combined day fees, reducing proportionately for a longer period, for access to all the records held – registration records, censuses, and parish registers, all in the same custody.

Certificates are much fuller, giving, e.g. dates of the marriage on a birth certificate, the names of both parents of the deceased on death certificates, even for aged persons, and the names of both parents on marriage certificates.

There was an amazing amount of detail in the certificates for 1855 itself. Birth certificates give the birthplace and ages of both parents, the date and place of marriage, and the number of previous children, whether living or dead. Marriage certificates give the birthplace, the names of both parents and the relationship, if any, of the couple. Death certificates sometimes give the spouse's name as well as the parents and place of burial as well.

It is possible, with good luck and stamina, to amass a full family tree to about 1800 in a day's intensive work. In the tourist season, crowds limit access to the Office, so get there early and be prepared to queue for seeing actual registers.

Paucity of surnames presents a problem, though. If all you know is that your John Macdonald came 'from Scotland', the multiplicity of choice may be overwhelming. Family Christian names may help, but some clue to a local area is really vital for certainty.

Ireland

General registration started in 1864, with records of Protestant (and some mixed) marriages from 1845. There is no single consolidated index, but entries from each county are filed together. It is thus difficult to find an ancestor, even after 1864, if your only clue is that he came 'from Ireland'. All records from 1864 to 1922 are held in Dublin, at the Office of the Registrar General, Joyce House, 8–11 Lombard Street, Dublin 2. After 1922, all southern Irish (Eire) records are held by Dublin, and those for Northern Ireland at The General Register Office, Oxford House, 49–55 Chichester Street, Belfast BT1 4HL.

From Dublin, certificates cost £2.25, which includes a search covering five years (two each side of the year you state) and a county of origin at least will be required. From Belfast, certificates cost £3.50, including a five-year search fee of £1.25, and they will require much more exact details, of place and parentage, which you will very probably not have. Dublin is less sticky that way, but very slow. Local registrars have been tried with no success at all by post, since they demand all the details you will get on the certificate, which you would not need if you had them.

Surnames are much more limited in Ireland and there is little hope of finding an ancestor of a common name if the only information is a vague age and a census birthplace stated as 'Ireland'. Somewhere in the family there may be a folk memory of a county. Rarer surnames can be located through Griffiths' *Primary Valuation of Tenements*, 1848–64 (available mainly in Ireland, but the Society of Genealogists has a microfiche copy) or perhaps from McLysaght's *Irish Family Names*.

Details on certificates are roughly the same as English information.

Short certificates

These are practically useless for genealogical purposes, giving date and place of birth only. They were introduced as a cheaper form of proof of age and to conceal details of illegitimate birth from the eyes of the curious.

Adoptions

Adoption certificates show the date of birth, but the names of the adopting parents, not the natural ones. Ask around the family for clues – it is the best source, but handled tactfully. In certain circumstances, information about the original parentage can be obtained through the official channels, but after counselling and careful examination of motives. There were no formal adoption certificates before 1927, and here the only source is the family or private orphanage and similar records. Some 'adopters' were very close relatives. A form to apply for information about the origins of an adopted child since 1927 can be obtained from St Catherine's, but only by the person concerned.

It isn't there!

General

1. *Yes it is*, but not in the spelling you use now. Spelling didn't settle until well after 1870. The poor, many of them illiterate, had to accept the version the parson, clerk or registrar preferred. Try every variant you can think of (dry-cleaners' English is a good guide) including changing the first vowel, e.g. Randell/el/ill/oll, Randle, Rendall/ill/oll/ull, Rondal, Rendle, Rondle, Rundall/dle, Rawndell, Raundle, etc. Adding or substracting an initial 'H' can take you into a different index book (Hammond, Ammon, Aman). The name Osborn has about 57 varieties, including Usborne, Asburn, Husborne, Orsborn, Horseborn – so use your imagination. Each spelling is indexed in strict alphabetical order in the indexes.

2. *Yes it is*, but mis-spelled entirely, not even as it sounds, by a deaf person or short-sighted copyist. This is more difficult. Watch out for a rare name converted to a common one roughly like it; for altered middle

letters, from bad hearing, or not crossing a 't', etc; for change of the first letter by slow listeners. For intance, Pattinson could turn up as Patterson, Batti(n)son, Passingham, Pakington, Matteson, Rallinson – and vice-versa. Try saying the name, or scribbling it down and getting a stranger to repeat or read it, to get an idea of possible errors. There was not a lot of difference between capital T, I, J and even F last century in some hands.

3. *Yes it is*, but the person changed his name later for a legacy inheritance (should show in wills) or to dodge the police, his wife, or the army. Try to catch him 'on the turn' in a census; reversion to claim a pension or later legacy; family hints; deathbed confessions, etc. Often a dodger will stick to the first name, or the same initials and the new name bears some relation to the old (Black to White, Robert Williams to William Roberts etc).

4. *No it isn't.* Some ancestors gave entirely false information on a birth or marriage certificate, which invalidates the next step. Try a census check, the electoral roll, school registers, etc – don't be beaten by a mere ancestor! Someone local probably shopped him at some time and even the most consistent liars leave traces somewhere.

Births

5. *Yes it is*, but not in the quarter you expect. If someone was born in March, he might not be registered until April, which brings the entry into the June quarter. December or even November babies may not appear till the next year, March quarter.

6. *Yes it is*, but not in the year you expect. People often know the day and month of birth, but not the year (even their own). Try the same quarter the year after, then the year before, and work outwards till you come to the name. Ages at death are very often wrong, so don't rely on them for finding birth dates. Ages at censuses can be pretty wild too – collect every age reference and try each date.

7. *Yes it is*, but the baby was registered in the maiden name of the mother and later adopted the name of its legal father, after the marriage. Sometimes the name of a step-father or legal guardian would be assumed, rarely with any formalities.

8. *Yes it is*, even in the right year and quarter, but Mother wanted to call the baby Algernon and Grandma wanted William Henry after Grandpa, and Father's only recommendation seemed to be Nelly Dean, so they registered him without a name – and he appears at the end of the list as 'male' only, after Zilpah.

9. *No it isn't.* A lot of births, in the first few decades after 1837, did not get registered. It was up to the Registrar to ask, not the parent to volunteer. Dissenters in particular refused and itinerants, dwellers in remote places or crowded cities like London, continued to avoid the registrar until 1940, when no registration meant no ration book.

10. *No it isn't*, at least, not in the standard St Catherine's indexes. He was born in Scotland, Ireland or abroad. Try the Miscellaneous indexes.

Marriages

11. *Yes it is*, but in the 'wrong' year. Start searching in the quarter when the known baby was born, work back. If no trace, forward. Some couples didn't get around to it until the day before the baby arrived, or after the second, fourth . . . fourteenth.

12. *Yes it is*, but in the 'wrong' place. They lived in Yorkshire but married in Kent, because she was in service, he in the army etc.

13. *Yes it is*, but the mother's name on the birth certificate is not the one she married under. If she was illegitimate, the parson might insist on a reversion to her name at birth, even if she was always known by another one. If she was a widow, then she would marry in that surname, but if asked her maiden name when registering a birth, would not necessarily volunteer the first married one. This might appear when a sibling was registered or be found in a census entry where half-kin were present.

14. *No it isn't* – they married in Scotland, Ireland or abroad. Try Miscellaneous indexes, especially Army records.

15. *No it isn't* – they never married. There was a lot of it about, especially in large towns.

Deaths

16. *Yes it is*, if it occurred in England and Wales, since registration was necessary to get a burial certificate for disposal. The only exception is likely to be an infant child, where the body could easily be buried. Try the wrong spelling, the wrong year, the wrong place – that is, wrong against your family information. Slightly wrong ages are common.

17. *No it isn't*. He died at sea or abroad. Try the Miscellaneous indexes. If he died in Scotland, see that Section – and lucky old you, since the information is likely to be so much fuller. If someone dies overseas with property in England, the name and exact date of death will appear in wills indexed at Somerset House, from 1858.

18. *Yes and no*. If a widow marries again, her death will appear in the new surname. Occasionally, a divorced or separated woman will revert to her maiden name, or assume another by deed poll or repute, and be registered in this name.

Missing entries

19. Especially in the early years, clergy sometimes failed to forward marriage registers and local registrars failed to forward all their entries. If you know the likely area, it may be worth trying the local registrar. This also overcomes problems due to mis-reading by London clerks and consequent bad mis-indexing.

Miscellaneous returns

At St Catherine's House, there are also indexes of events which happened to British subjects abroad or those who were serving in the armed forces. They do not form a complete record of Britons abroad, since only those events registered by the Consul or the services' authorities are included and some of the latter are not fully indexed. The indexes which exist are shelved in the search room in the first bay on the left after the stairs. Each index is labelled on the spine and they contain:

Army Chaplains' Registers: Births 1760–1955; Marriages 1796–1955; Deaths 1761–1970.
War Deaths: South Africa 1899–1902.
          Army Officers 1914–1921; 1939–1945.
          Army Other Ranks 1914–1921; 1939–45.
          Naval Officers 1914–1921; 1939–1945.
          Navy Other Ranks 1914–1921; 1939–1945.
          Royal Air Force 1939–1945.
Consular births, Miscellaneous, 1849–1965.
HM Ships – Marriages 1849–1889.
Marriages abroad, Miscellaneous, 1946–1970s.
UK Commonwealth Marriages, 1947–1965.
Marine deaths (ie at sea, not HM Marines), 1837–1965.
Consular deaths, 1849–1965.
Deaths abroad, 1951–1970s.
UK High Commission deaths, 1950–1965.
Deaths in the air, 1945–1970s.

Entries from these registers are applied for on special forms, and by special procedures. If you find one which you think will be useful, consult one of the officials on duty, who will show you what to write down.

Don't be surprised not to find your ancestor. Not all soldiers married with permission or had their children 'on the strength'. Not all Britons abroad bothered to register with a distant consul – which causes problems for descendants wishing to settle here. Additional, semi-indexed, – records are held upstairs at St Catherine's.

Miscellaneous Foreign Registers

Also on the Miscellaneous shelves are indexes to the registers kept by clergymen who ministered to the British community abroad. Some of these are very old.

Belgium	Baptisms, burials, 1817–1850.
Burma	Baptisms, burials, 1817–1850.
China	Baptisms, marriages, burials, 1899–1945.
Denmark	Marriages, 1853–1874.
France	Births, marriages, burials, 1815–1895 (Boulogne, Paris, Rouen, Havre, Calais).
Germany	Births, marriages, burials, 1817–1895 (Dresden, Hanover).

Holland	Births, marriages, burials, 1627–1894 (The Hague, Rotterdam).
India	Births, marriages, burials, 1894–1947.
Italy	Births, marriages, burials, 1840–1947 (Naples, Rome, Venice, Turin, Florence).
Japan	Births, marriages, burials, 1874–1941.
Mesopotamia	Births, marriages, burials, 1915–1931.
Palestine	Births, burials, 1920–1931.
Portugal	Births, marriages, burials, 1814–1874.
Roumania	Marriages, 1868–1914.
Russia	Births, marriages, burials, 1840–1918.
Sweden	Marriages, 1845–1891.

These entries apply only to the British communities in these countries, and not necessarily all of them. The original registers are held by the Public Record Office, Chancery Lane, where they can be seen by searchers (Reader's Ticket required) without any charge.

General advice

Don't dress in your best bib and tucker – those books are dirty and heaving them around is sweaty.

Don't take a load of shopping – there isn't room.

Don't take the kids – unless they are keen to help.

Don't expect instant success – but don't give up.

Do put the index books back in the right place again.

Do watch your handbag or wallet.

Don't believe that they can't make a mistake, they can, they have, they always did and always will.

Getting your number?

You may not know which district your ancestral village comes into. Don't despair – the Enquiry Desk has a complete list of even the smallest hamlets and their district. You may find a likely ancestor in a Registration District you have never heard of. Again, you could find out where it is from the list. However, to save constant trips to the desk, the area code – the figure which appears immediately after the district – is a useful clue. This figure applies to one county or group of adjacent areas, and your ancestral family could be anywhere in one code area, or move into adjacent ones.

These codes were in Roman numerals from 1837 to 1851 and then in arabic numerals with letter subdivisions till 1946. The lower the number, the nearer London or further south.

I; 1a, *1b	London (Bloomsbury, St George Hanover Square, *St Giles, St Marylebone, *St Pancras, Westminster; St Martin, Strand)
II; *1b,1c,**1d	London (City, **Bermondsey, Bethnal Green, *Holborn, Mile End, **Newington, Poplar, **Rotherhithe, Stepney, Whitechapel)
III; *1a,**1b,3a	Middlesex (*Chelsea, *Clerkenwell, *Fulham, **Hackney, *Kensington, *Hampstead, **Islington, rest of Middlesex)
IV; *1d,2a	Surrey (*Camberwell, *Lambeth, *Southwark, *Wandsworth, rest of Surrey)
V; *1d,2a	Kent (*Greenwich, *Lewisham, *Woolwich, rest of Kent)
VI; 3a,*3b	*Bedfordshire, Berkshire, Buckinghamshire and Hertfordshire
VII;*2c	Sussex, East Hampshire (*Excl. Portsmouth)
VIII;*2b	S.W. Hampshire (*and Portsmouth area)
VIII; 5a	Dorset, Wiltshire
IX; 5c	Cornwall
§IX, X; 5b	Devon (§Plymouth, §Totnes, §Tavistock)
X, §XI, 5c	Somerset (§Bath, §Clutton, §Keynsham)
XI, §XVI; 6a	Gloucestershire (§Westbury on Severn)
XII; 4a	Essex and South Suffolk
XIII; 4b	Norfolk and North Suffolk
XIV; 3b	Cambridgeshire, Huntingdonshire
XIV; 7a	Lincolnshire
XV; 7a	Leicestershire, Northamptonshire, Rutland
XV; 7b	Nottinghamshire
XVI; *3a,6d	*Oxfordshire, Warwickshire
XVII; 6b	Staffordshire
XVIII; 6a,*6c	*Worcestershire, Shropshire
XIX; *8a, 7b	*Cheshire, Derbyshire
XX; 8b,*8c,**8d	South Lancashire (Liverpool, West Derby, Prescot; *Barton, *Chorlton, *Warrington; **Ashton, **Manchester, **Oldham, **Prestwich, **Salford)
XXI; *8b,**8c,8e	Rest of Lancashire (*Ormskirk; **Bolton, **Bury, **Leigh, **Wigan); (Todmorden 9a)
§XXI,XXII; *9a,9c	South Yorkshire (West Riding) to Wakefield (§*Halifax, §*Saddleworth, *Huddersfield)
§XXII, XXIII; 9a,*9b,**9c	Rest of Yorkshire West Riding (*Leeds area, *Bradford, §*Dewsbury; **Bramham, **Selby, **Tadcaster)
XXIII; 9d	Yorkshire East Riding (Hull, Beverley, Howden etc)
§XXIII,XXIV; 9d	Yorkshire North Riding (§Aysgarth)
XXIV; 10a	County Durham
XXV; 10b, *8e	Cumberland, Northumberland, Westmorland; (Lancashire: *Barrow in Furness, *Ulverstone)
XXVI; 6a	Herefordshire; Westbury, Glos.
XXVI; 11a	Carmarthen, Glamorgan, Monmouth, Pembroke
§XXVI,XXVII; 11b	Rest of Wales (§Brecknock, §Radnor)

Detailed maps of Registration Districts 1837–51 and 1852–1946 are available from the Institute of Heraldic and Genealogical Studies, Northgate, Canterbury.

Local copies of the GRO indexes

Copies are available on microfilm or more recently on microfiche. Sets, (or part sets mainly concentrating on the nineteenth century), can be consulted in various provincial locations, of which the following list covers most of the publicly accessible ones. No one else but the Registrar General has copies of all the actual registers. Obtain individual certificates from the local registrar for the area named, or get a friend or agent (for a small fee if you provide the reference) to order the certificate in London. Postal orders to St Catherine's (dealt with from Southport) cost at least twice the basic fee.

LONDON area:

Society of Genealogists' Library,
14 Charterhouse Buildings,
Goswell Rd., EC1M 7BA.
C1837–1920 (members or small fee for use, closed Mon. open Sats).

Ilford Redbridge Central Library,
Clements Rd., Ilford IG1 1EA
BMD 1866–1912 (+).

SOUTH OF ENGLAND/HOME COUNTIES

Aylesbury Local Studies Lib., Ref. Lib.,
Walton St. BMD 1837–1983

Basingstoke Ref. Lib. BMD 1837–1983

Bromley Local Studies, Cent. Lib., High St
BR1 1EX
(tel 0181 460 9955) BMD 1837–1983
book 1 week ahead for 1hr.

Hertford Local Studies Lib, Reg. Office
Block, County Hall SGD13 8EJ (tel
01992–556624) BMD 1837–1983
booking 1 week ahead.

Oxford Local Studies Lib., Westgate. (tel
01865 815749) BMD 1837–1983
booking advisable

Portsmouth Ref. Library B1866–1983 must
book

Hampshire FHS BMD 1837–1900
(members)

WEST COUNTRY

Bristol Central Library, College Green
BS1 5TL (tel 01272 276121)
BMD 1837–1983 must book

Redruth Local Studies Lib. County
Library, Clinton Rd., Redruth
TR15 2QE (tel 01209 216760)
BM 1866–1939 Booking advised

MIDLANDS

Birmingham Central Library (History
Dept.) Chamberlain Square,
Birmingham B3 3HQ (tel 0121 235
4549) BMD 1837–1930 gtd booking at
50p per hour or take chance

Cambridge C.R.O. Shire Hall, Castle Hill
CB3 0AP (tel 01223 317281)
BMD 1837–1912

Cheltenham Mormon FH Centre BMD
1837–1910 + some later. (see FHC list)

Dudley Local His. Lib., Mount Pleasant
St., Coseley BMD 1837–1920 Not
Mon, (1 + 3 Sats pre order) (tel 01902
880011) book £1/4 hrs

Hereford CRO Old Barracks, Harrold St.
BMD 1866–1916

Leicester FHS B1837–1900 members only

Matlock Local Studies Cty. Libr., County
Offices. BMD 1837–65(+) (tel 01629
580000 ext 6840)

Smethwick Sandwell Pub. Lib. (tel 0121
588 0497) BMD 1881–1920 Booking

Walsall L Hist. Centre, Essex St W52 7AS
(tel 01922 72130516) BMD 1837–1950
book; not Mon

Wolverhampton L Studies, Cent. Lib.,
Snow Hill (tel 01902 312025) BMD
1837–1983 Book; 50p hr

Worcester CRO, Cty. Hall, Spetchley Rd.
WR5 2NP (tel 01905 353366)
BMD 1837–1983 Book.

EAST ANGLIA

Felixstowe FHS B1891–1900 (members)

Norwich Central Lib., Bethel St. (tel 01603
219080) 1837–1910 (temp unavailable
1995 after fire)

LANCASHIRE

Liverpool Record Office, Brown, Picton &

Hornby Library, William Brown St
L3 8EW (tel 0151 207 2147) BMD
1837–1912

Manchester C.R.O. 56 Marshall St., New
Cross M4 5FU (tel 0161 247 3383)
BMD 1837–1912 Booking essential,
3 hr periods

St Helens Local History & Archives,
Century House, Hardshaw St.,
St Helens WA10 1RN (tel 01744 24061)
BMD 1837–1940 Book pref

Preston Central Library, Market Square.
PR1 2PP (tel 01772 53191)
BMD 1866–1912 Book pref

YORKSHIRE

Huddersfield Local Studies Dept., Kirklees
Central Lib., Princess Alexandra Walk,
(tel 01484 513808) BMD 1837–1912

Hull Humberside Libraries, St Andrews,
Bakers Hill, Hull, BMD 1837–1983

Leeds Reference Dept. Central Library,
Municipal Buildings, Leeds LS1 3AB
(tel 01532 462016) BMD 1837–1980

Northallerton Library, Grammar School
Lane, Northallerton DL6 1PT (tel
01609 6271) BMD 1837–1946. Booking
preferred

Sheffield Archives, 52 Shoreham St. BMD
1837–93. Not Fri. Booking

York Central Library, Local History
Dept., Museum St., York Y01 2DS (tel
01904 55631)

NORTH EAST

Morpeth Northumberland County Library,
The Willows, Morpeth NE61 1TA (tel
01670 512385) BMD 1837–1918

Newcastle on Tyne Central Library,
Princess Sq., NE99 1DX (0191-261
0691) BMD 1837–1983

South Shields South Tyneside Central
Library, Prince George Square, S.
Shields NE33 2PE (tel 0191 471 4351)
BMD 1837–1925 Book Sat.

WALES

Aberystwyth National Library of Wales,
SY23 3BU (tel 01970 623816) BMD
1837–1983 Reader's ticket in advance.

Cardiff CRO Cty Hall, Cathays Park CF1
3NE (tel 01222 820284) BMD 1837–
1983 Not Mon. Book

Mold Clwyd Library H.Q. Civic Centre.
Mold, CH7 6NW (tel 01352 2121) BMD
1837–1930 Book

Swansea CRO, County Hall, Oystermouth
Rd., Swansea SA1 3SN (tel 01792
471589) BMD 1837–1983 Mon–Wed +
Wed evng. Charge 50p per hour. Book

SCOTLAND GRO Edingburgh EH1 3YT
(tel 0131 556 3952) BMD 1837–1983
Access for holders of Search Pass only.

AUSTRALIA

Most major family history societies either
have or will be obtaining at least part of
the indexes. I therefore include
addresses so that the current position
may be checked with them.

A.C.T. Her. & Gen. Soc. of Canberra Inc.,
PO Box 585, Canberra, ACT 2601

N.S.W. Soc. of Aust. Genealogists,
Richmond Villa, 120 Kent St.,
Observatory Hill, Sydney NSW 2000

Northern Territory Gen Soc. of Northern
Territory, PO Box 37212, Winnellie,
NT 5789

Queensland Qld FHS, PO Box 171,
Indooropilly, Brisbane 4068: Gen. Soc.
of QLD, PO Box 423 Woolloongabba,
QLD 4102

South Australia S. Aust. Gen. & Her. Soc.,
PO Box 592, Adelaide, S. Australia
5001

Tasmania Gen. Soc. of Tasmania, PO Box
60, Prospect, Tas. 7250

Victoria Aust. Instit. Genealogical Studies,
PO Box 68, Oakleigh, Victoria 3166

Western Australia WA Gen. Soc. Inc.,
5/48 May St., Bayswater WA 6053

CANADA

Saskatchewan Gen. Soc. 1870 Lorne St.,
Regina, S4P 2L7

Ontario Ontario GS, Suite 251, 70 Orchard
View Bvd, Toronto M4R 1B9

NEW ZEALAND

Auckland Public Library

Lower Hall Gen. Research Inst. of NZ,
PO Box 36-107, Moera, Lower Hutt

U.S.A.

Salt Lake City Fam. Hist. Center, Church
of Jesus Christ of Latter Day Saints, 50
East No Temple, Salt Lake City, Utah
84150 (and branch FHCs)

Mormon Family History Centres

Films of St Catherine's BMD indexes, the Scottish and Irish BMD indexes, (and much else) can be seen at any LDS Family History Centre. A few Centres* actually hold all/part of St Catherine's indexes in stock and the other centres can obtain them from the USA for a fee of £3.50 a microfilm roll (though long searches involves many rolls). An alternative BMD copy in a public library near you would be a better bet. Once obtained, the films are held for a month. If no phone number is stated, the centre is likely to be new and small, but may grow rapidly. No charge is made, except for obtaining films of records not held in stock.

Aberdeen North Anderson Dr. AB2 6DD (tel 01224 692206)

Aldershot St George's Rd (tel 01252 21460)

Ashton under Lyne Tweedale St, Rock Dale (tel 01706 526292)

Belfast 401 Holywood Rd BT4 2GU (tel 01232 768250)

*Billingham, Cleveland, The Linkway TS23 3HJ (tel 01642 563162)

Blackpool Warrem Drive FY5

Bristol 721 Wells Rd, Whitchurch BS14 9HU (tel 01179 83836)

Cambridge 670 Cherry Hinton Rd CB1 4DR (tel 01223 247010)

Canterbury Forty Acre Rd (tel 01227 451567)

Cardiff Heol y Deri, Rhibwina, S Glam CF4 6UH (tel 01222 620205)

Carlisle Langrigg Rd, Morton Park (tel 01228 26767)

*Cheltenham Thirlestaine Rd GL53 7AA (tel 01242 523433)

Chester 30 Cliftone Drive, Blacon CH1 5LT (tel 01244 390 796)

Chorley 33–41 Walter St, Chorley (tel 012572 69332)

Coleford, Forest of Dean: Wynols Hill, Queensway

Cork (Munster)pending; enquiries via Dublin

Coventry Riverside Close, Whitley (tel 01203 301420)

*Crawley Sussex, Old Horsham Rd RH11 8PD (tel 01293 516151)

Douglas IOM Woodside, Woodburn Rd (tel 01624 75834)

Dublin The Willows, Finglas, Dublin 11 (tel 010 3531 8309960)

Dumfries 36 Edinburgh Rd, Albanybank

Dundee Bingham Terrace, DD4 7HH (tel 01382 451247)

Edinburgh 30a Colinton Rd, E10 (tel 0131 337 3049)

Elgin Pansport Rd Elgin, Moray

Glasgow 35 Julian Ave G12 0RB (tel 0141 357 1024)

Grimsby Linwood Ave, Waltham Rd

Harborne 38 Lordswood Rd, B17 9QS (tel 0121 427 9291)

Helston Clodgey Lane

Hornchurch, 64 Butts Green Rd (tel 01424 58412)

*Huddersfield 2 Halifax St, Birchencliffe (tel 01484 420352)

Hull 752 Holderness Rd, (tel 01482 572623)

Inverness 13 Ness Walk IV3 5QS

Ipswich 42 Sidegate Lane West IP4 3DB (tel 01473 723182)

Jersey Rue de la Vallee, St Mary, St Helier, CI. (tel 01534 82171)

Kilmarnock Whatriggs Rd KA1 3QY

Kirkcaldy Winifred Cres, Forth Pk (tel 01592 640041)

Lancaster Ovangle Rd LA1

Leeds Vesper Rd LS5 (tel 0113 258 5297)

Lerwick South Rd (tel 01595 5732)

Lichfield Purcell Ave WS17 7P (tel 01543 414843)

Limerick Doraddoyle Rd, Limerick

Lincoln Skellingthorpe Rd LN6 0OP

*Liverpool 4 Mill Bank Rd, L13 0BW (tel 0151 228 0433)

*London 64/68 Exhibition Rd,
S Kensington SW7 2PA (reopens cApr
1995, check with 0171 370 7866/0171
938 1330 or fax 0171 589 8561)

London 149 Nightingale Lane, Balham,
SW12 (tel 0181 673 6741)
('Wandsworth')

Londonderry Racecourse Rd, Belmont

*Loughborough Thorpe Hill, Alan
Moss Rd (tel 01509 214991)
('Leicester')

Lowestoft 165 Yarmouth Rd NR32

Luton corner London Rd/Cutenhoe Rd (tel
01582 482234) ('St Albans')

Maidstone 76b London Rd ME16 0DR (tel
01622 757811)

Manchester Altrincham Rd, Wythen-
shawe M22 4BJ (tel 0161 902 9279)

Mansfield Southridge Drive NG18 4FT (tel
01623 26729)

Merthyr Tydfil Nantygwenith Rd,
Georgetown (tel 01685 722455)

*Newcastle under Lyme Staffs; PO Box
285, The Brampton (tel 01782 620653)

Newport IOW Chestnut Close, Shide Rd
(tel 01983 529643)

Northampton 137 Harlestone Rd NN5 (tel
01604 51348)

Norwich 19 Greenways, Eaton NR4 7AX
(tel 01603 52440)

Nottingham Hempshill Lane, Bulwell
NG6 8PA (tel 0115-927-4194)

Paisley Campbell St, Johnstone PA5 8LD
(tel 01505 20886)

Peterborough Cottesmore Cl., Atherstone
Ave, Netherton Estate (tel 01733
263374)

Plymouth Hartley Chapel, Mannamead Rd
PL3 (tel 01752 668666)

Poole 8 Mount Rd, Parkstone BH14 0QW
(tel 01202 730646)

Portsmouth Kingston Crescent (tel 01705
969243)

Rawtenstall Haslington Rd (tel 01706
213460)

Reading 280 The Meadway, Tilehurst (tel
01734 410211)

Redditch 321 Evesham Rd, Crabbs Cross
(tel 01527 550657)

Rhyl Rhuddlan Rd, Rhyl

Rochdale Tweedale St, OL11 3TZ (tel
01706 526292)

Scarborough Stepheny Dr, Whitby Rd

Sheffield Wheel Lane, Grenoside S30 3RL
(tel 0114-245-3231)

Staines 41 Kingston Rd TW14 0ND (tel
01784 453823)

Stevenage Buckthorn Ave (tel 01438
351553)

Sunderland Linden Rd, Queen Alexandra
Rd (tel 01915 285787)

*Sutton Coldfield 185 Penns Lane (tel 0121
384 2028)

Swansea Cockett Rd, Swansea

Telford 72 Glebe St, Wellington

Thetford Station Rd (tel 01842 5472)

Wednesfield Linthouse Lane,
Wolverhampton

Worthing Goring Rd (tel 01903 241829)

Yate, Avon: Wellington Rd (tel 01454
323004)

Yeovil Forest Hill Chapel

York West Bank, Acomb (tel 01904
798185)

(list kindly supplied by the LDS Family Service Centre, Sutton Coldfield, Birmingham)

Scottish GRO indexes

A microfilm of 1855 (complete) 1856–1920 (indexes) is held by the Society of Genealogists, 14 Charterhouse Buildings, Goswell Rd, London EC1M 7BA. It may be used by non-members for a hourly/daily fee. (Tues–Sat). Major Mormon Family History Centres in London, Birmingham and Cheltenham etc also hold copies of the Scottish GRO indexes to (BM) 1920 (Deaths to 1930). They also have the Irish BD 1864–1921 and M 1845–1930 indexes, freely available. Other FHCs can order all these.

Many Births and Marriages for Scotland 1855–75 are included in the International Genealogical Index, extensively available in public librar-ies or Record Offices etc. A precise date from the IGI can be used to apply for the full certificate from the Registrar General for Scotland,

Register House, Edinburgh 1 and is normally sent within a few days. Postal applicants lacking such a date will need to send as many identifying details as possible. There could be many James Stewarts born in 1890 or so 'in Scotland' – try to help locate him in a town or area. The Scottish GRO are very thorough, but miracles are extra.

What do I do with these certificates?

The object of getting certificates is not to paper your walls or donate untold gold to the government, but to further your research. Unless you are claiming a peerage or a fortune, you don't need paper proof of every step. If the family say Jack was born on 10 August 1909 and he is registered in SEPT quarter 1909, you can accept that. You may want certificates for all your direct ancestors, but the cost soon mounts up and it may make sense instead to buy one for a sibling of your ancestor which will give you an address for the next stage, searching the census. For instance, your father told you he was born in Handley, which you find by asking at the enquiry desk is in Newchurch registration district (RD). He and his family are registered there. But the next generation, including his father, Andrew (1875), and his known uncle, Harry (1871) were born in Oldchurch RD, covering two small towns and a dozen villages. It has the same area number, so it is not far away. But which town or village is it? You could search the whole district in 1871 for a Bloggs family with an infant named Harry, which won't take too long for each village. In an urban area, though, the search takes longer; get Harry's certificate, and go straight to the right place, Sprotley. A large city is really impractical to search without a street address, London impossible. The certificate saves the cost of more trips to search the census, and gives you parents' names for getting the marriage certificate too.

Using directories to find an address

In some cases, you may be able to find an address in a directory, if the ancestor was wealthy or in trade in his own right. A one-man business is included, but not necessarily the foreman of a large works with twenty men under him. A few town directories are more comprehensive, with most residents, but almost never the place you need. 'Ancestral' libraries have the best run of directories for their own area. Counties may have combined-directories listing neighbouring areas (e.g. Berks, Bucks and Oxon). The Guildhall Library (open Mon–Sat, free) has all London ones, as you would expect, and also the finest collection of some for the whole country in one place. The Census Office has directories for census years only for a number of places. The Society of Genealogists also has a countrywide collection, of which a list is published.

If you know the occupation of your ancestor, and he doesn't figure in the directories, note anyone of the same surname in the same occupation. It could be the father or uncle he worked for and lived close to.

THE CENSUSES, 1841–1881
Their Use and Interpretation

The census

When people talk about 'consulting the census' they normally mean the returns of the censuses of the population of England and Wales taken in 1841, 1851, 1861, 1871, 1881, 1891, which are now open to public inspection in England, Wales and Scotland. In Ireland, so little survives from the nineteenth century that the census does not exist as a practical research tool, though part of the 1901 and 1911 censuses is available for search. All other census returns are withheld from inspection under the hundred year secrecy rule.

What is the census?

There had been earlier counts of the population, but none were made regularly until 1801. Only in 1841 did the Government decide it needed more than the numbers of people in the various age groups. Reaction was sharp and unfavourable, on theological grounds from those who believed that 'numbering the people' was blasphemous, and on more practical grounds from a suspicion that the object was to extract more taxes, force a resettlement of poor people or their emigration, or just plain getting to know too much about the private individual. The amount of information to be collected was therefore restricted, and instead of sending strangers from London, local residents were appointed as 'enumerators'. The idea was partly that they would get more co-operation, partly that they would know more of what was required anyway, so false information would be detected at source.

The 1841 census

In June 1841, the population of each village, town or city, and even of tiny hamlets and isolated farms, was to be listed, household by house-hold, and every person, resident or temporary visitor, written down, with the *name* of each person, not just the head, their *sex* and their *ages* also, to the nearest multiple of five years below, in the case of adults, and exactly for children up to 15; their *occupations*; and their *birthplaces* – but only whether or not they were born in the county where they now lived. There was also a space to indicate if they were born in 'Scotland, Ireland or Foreign Parts' (or, in Scotland, 'England, Ireland or Foreign Parts').

In practice, many of these details were omitted or incorrect. In districts where few people could write, or where opposition was par-ticularly militant, the enumerator often took the easy way out and filled in the forms himself, from personal knowledge and more or less good guesswork. Occupations were often given only for the head of the household and non-related males, and birthplaces were sometimes filled in with a consistent 'Y' for 'Yes, born in county' except for obvious aliens like clergymen and visiting gentry.

The worst inaccuracies came in the stated ages. Some enumerators never got the hang of 'multiples of five' and put the exact ages they were given. Others used the multiple of five *above* the correct age. Most did their best with the system laid down, but were led astray by ages given them incorrectly. Some errors were deliberate, others through lack of knowledge on the part of the person or the head of the family of what a man's true age was. If he was 42, the age should have gone down as 40; if he thought he was 39, he was entered as 35 – a sizeable error.

Birthplaces were often given as 'in the county' when they were not, because the persons, especially if old and poor, feared to be sent back to their 'home' if they admitted coming as an immigrant sixty years back. If a village was close to a county boundary, then someone born a hundred yards down the road should have been entered as 'N', while an incomer from the other end of the county, thirty miles or more away, was entered as 'Y' and so looked more local. Some boundaries passed right through the middle of the house, and so brothers born in different bedrooms would be 'N' and 'Y' at the same address, without ever moving. People loved exploiting these little anomalies, if it mucked up the official system.

Households are normally set out in 'natural order' with father first, then mother and the children, then other relatives, servants, employees, lodgers and visitors – but no relationships are stated, so the searcher may be misled by the unusual combinations, of brother and sister, nieces and nephews, etc.

The 1851 and subsequent censuses

In spring 1851 and later, the amount of information demanded was stepped up. The opposition remained vociferous, but the majority were resigned to the decennial inquisition. A few middle-class intellectuals used great ingenuity to avoid enumeration, by travelling overnight, or complied with the letter of the law, but not the spirit, by stating their birthplaces as the county or even the country only, and by using initials instead of full names.

Ages. These now had to be given correctly. Some people gave wrong information on principle, but many more through lack of knowledge, and some enumerators still had to make guesses for the bewildered or unco-operative, and used round figures based on the five year steps of 1841. There may be strange discrepancies over the five decades when censuses were taken.

Birthplaces. These were also to be given exactly. The same supicions by the poor that they would be evicted applied. Many people really didn't know where they were born, especially the eldest of a family, since the family moved when they were toddlers and 'always lived here' ever since. Richer folk are either very detailed or maddeningly reticent, giving 'London' as a birthplace, which is pretty useless for tracing pre-1837 events among hundreds of parishes.

Occupations. These were given for everyone. Tradesmen were defined as 'master', 'journeyman' or 'apprentice' and the number of employees of a master stated. Farmers gave acreage and number of employees, by sex. Even children had their own occupations – many were gainfully employed at tender ages. Those at school or not employed were 'scholars' and this occupation is often given for infants of a few days old. Small babies may be unnamed, or sometimes a name is filled in for a tiny infant which is thought better of later. Prevalent occupations locally are abbreviated.

Relationships of all residents to the head of the household were stated for the first time, combined with marital status (single, married, widow/er). This caused great upset to couples living together without benefit of clergy, frightened by threats of legal penalties into revealing all. The parentage of bastards is often made clear. Was the child 'son' or 'wife's son'? The latter relationship was often shown as 'son in law', the older version of stepson, though the phrase had the modern meaning too. A child brought up by grandparents as their own may be revealed as the child of an unmarried daughter, either by a knowing enumerator, or a family too timid to brazen it out. But beware the enumerator's own mistakes – where married children are living with their father, their own children easily may be described as 'son' or 'daughter' when it is clear from the context they should be 'grandson', etc.

There were classifications to cover other members of the household, including 'servants' (then described more exactly under 'occupation'), 'lodgers', 'visitors' – but there is very little room to describe a married son or daughter who had dropped in on the family at census night. Nevertheless, some enumerators squeezed both relationships into the tiny space.

Medical information.   There was a final column in which to make a note of anyone who was 'blind, deaf or idiot'. The duration of the ailment was sometimes stated and other medical problems might be included, in great detail. Incidentally, a tick in this column running all the way down the page does not mean that everyone in the household was afflicted in this way. It indicates that information has been abstracted by the statisticians after being sent in.

Some of these statisticians caused great problems by slapping their pencil ticks across ages or parts of names and occupations, which thus don't show clearly on film.

The 1851 census forms were filled-in in ink, so the films are generally more legible, though bad writing is a hazard and some cheap ink has faded with the years, before filming. An occasional problem is that ages, in particular, have been miscopied from the rough originals, and an '8' is found where a '6' might be expected, or a '4' for a '7' and vice-versa, so do not regard the enumeration book as Holy Writ.

Enumerators were also asked to list people not living in houses – vagrants, gipsies, travelling traders, railway navvies, boat people – and there were special forms for vessels in port, to be filled in by the master. The enumerator was asked to state how many normal inhabitants were absent and why, and to account for any noticeable increase or decrease in population. These details, at the end of the official pages of the books, form an interesting sidelight on local conditions.

Institutions, like prisons, workhouses, barracks and large schools, were enumerated in separate schedules attached to the place. Some enumerators for prisons and asylums use initials only for the inmates, which is annoying.

Where can they be seen?

The Censuses for the whole of England and Wales are kept by the Public Record Office, in London. The Census Rooms are currently in the basement of the Chancery Lane building. When other main records are transferred to Kew in 1996, it is intended to retain a Public

Microform Search Room in London which will still provide access to the censuses. The Rooms are open from Monday to Saturday 9.30 am to 5 pm.

Consultation is currently free and there are few formalities, other than signing a visitors' register. You may take a friend and even children over 10 actually helping, not running around the tables. At congested periods, you will queue upstairs (seats provided) until signalled to go downstairs. When you sign in, a numbered pass is allocated, and at slack times, you can ask for a seat in an area convenient for the census year you want to search. The 1891 census can be read on microfilm or microfiche. You will have to leave any oversize bags, including large handbags, in a locker, for which you need a (returnable) £1 coin. There are cloakrooms and a tearoom near the pass desk.

Local copies

If you live further from London than from the area you are researching, you will probably find it easier to consult local copies of the census films. These are held by local County Record Offices, Local Studies Departments or major libraries. The CRO or main County Library may have the census for the whole county may possibly not for all six census years. But they may also have films for adjacent parts of neighbouring counties, as registration areas often overlapped county boundaries. Town or area libraries may have films for a small local area only. The key to the extent and distribution of these locally-held copies is in *Census Returns 1841–91 on Microform* (Gibson Guide)

It is often necessary and always advisable to book the use of a microfilm reader beforehand – telephone to find out if this is possible. CROs may have only one or two, though many records may now be on film. Their opening hours may be restricted and a fee is sometimes charged for use of the machine or office.

Local Studies Departments and libraries stay open for much longer hours and may be better equipped with film readers. They can often be visited in the evening and, if you live locally enough, are practical to use for quite short periods at a time. Their readers are not always bookable, but, especially if you are travelling from a distance, you should find out.

As only a few films are involved, the system for selection and reading the one you want may be much less formal than the one given here for the PRO Census Room. Well-behaved children are tolerated cheerfully in most places, so this can be an ideal introduction for the school-children in holidays (though other people may have the same idea). Even babies will keep quiet for an hour or so (well, sometimes).

Above all, especially if you can book your reader, conditions are much less crowded and are generally more congenial – but, of course, you are restricted to the area the office or library serves, whilst at the PRO you can range from one part of the country to another. Copies of the census for 1891 on microfiche can be bought from the P.R.O. Reprographics Department, Ruskin Ave, Kew (ask for details). The minimum amount is a sub-district, which will cost from £8 for an average population, more for densely populated areas. This is a very useful facility, since you can study in depth at home or using a microfiche reader in a local library.

Before you start – where were they?

You cannot make use of the census returns until you know just where your ancestor(s) lived at the date. All returns are filed just as they were collected, county by county, parish by parish. Unless you know which parish they lived in in one census year, you can't even start hunting for the entry. Even within the parish, names are not filled in alphabetical order but in the households and family groups where they were living on one particular night.

You may be able to find the parish from family information – a traditional connection with a place has usually got something right about it, even if it is not one hundred per cent accurate. Official records help. Marriage certificates may say 'of this parish' only, but birth certificates give a more exact address. For families living in a village, this may be just the village name, which is enough, because most are small enough to search through in a short time.

Towns of any size are another matter. A street address is vital for town ancestors, especially those living in London or any major city – unless you are prepared to devote a long time to the work. You may obtain this from a certificate – and buying the birth certificate of a sibling, instead of the direct ancestor, may be necessary to get close to a census year. If your ancestor was well-to-do, he may appear in the 'Court' or 'Private' section of a town directory. If he was a tradesman in his own right, then he should figure in the 'Commercial' section – even if he only had a one-man business. Employees rarely occur, unless they were managers, who would rate as 'Private' residents, in the earlier directories. Even when a directory purports to be a street directory, it doesn't necessarily include every resident – only those who have indicated their willingness to pay for a copy.

In London and some other cities, people tended to move frequently, from one rented house to another as their finances improved or deteriorated. An address for 1860 or 1865 may get you nowhere in 1861 or 1871. Go armed with as many addresses as possible and one may work out.

There are directories for London in the census years, accessible in the Census Room by the indexes, but otherwise it pays to do your homework first, either among old directories in your local library, or, in London, in the Guildhall Library, which has the best general collection for the whole country, as well as superb coverage for London itself. The Society of Genealogists' library also has a useful collection.

The Index Room at Chancery Lane has colour coded books for each census year ranged round the walls. You will need to consult at least two books and possibly a street index as well. If you are looking for a village, find it in alphabetical order in Index One.

In 1841, there is a number against each place which leads to the page in Index Two. Here the counties are listed in alphabetical order, then grouped in the old administrative divisions called Hundreds. If you know your county and Hundred, you could go straight to this index. Your parish will be in alphabetical order in its hundred, with minor exceptions, where 'hamlets' are listed under the mother parish. Sometimes the hamlet later grew bigger than Mum, because it had some industry or the railway station. A few places – new town estates or mining villages – had not yet acquired their modern names by 1841, so a study of local history and maps will help.

You will see a number in the left-hand margin by it, which may cover half a dozen villages, or one medium sized town, or part of a city. This is your PIECE NUMBER which will get you your film.

In 1851, this simple system was changed. The first index is alphabetical and has two numbers by each parish or hamlet. This leads in a devious way to the second index. Here the counties are now all grouped in strangely-conceived geographical areas, and subdivided into Poor Law Unions, roughly the same as Registration Districts. The Unions are numbered consecutively in **heavy type** through the book and the first number in the first index leads you to the Union. Each Union has sub-districts, and the second number leads to these, where you will find your village and the Piece Number against it in the margin. This system has continued with very minor modifications, even for the 1881 census, where it was hoped a single index could be used for direct reference.

It is necessary to use the first index to find your numbers, since some Unions cross county boundaries and your village may not be in its own county at all, even if you can trace this.

Town street indexes

For large towns and cities, there may be several films covering one town, or, in the case of London, one section of the city. Fortunately, street indexes have been made, by the officials and others, to London and most major cities and even provincial towns. These are shelved with the indexes for censuses they cover and bound in the same colour. Some older indexes are on cards in a cabinet nearby. This is noted in the main index book. It helps to know which general area a London street should be in – there are a lot of West Streets and Church Roads. You can get the borough or parish from certificates or town directories.

The street index will give a reference which will either lead back to the second index or will be 'translated' at the front of each small section. The enumeration district numbers also given help locate the exact part of the film needed. It is often rather difficult to pick out which of the numbers scribbled on the front of each enumerator's 'book' is meant.

Long streets in towns were divided between several enumerators, who did a section plus the side roads. Thus one street may appear on several films, which may mean a lot of searching, if you don't know the precise house number.

Other indexes

Local repositories may have their own form of indexing, sometimes renumbering the reels of film. In some cases, not only street but partial surname indexes may be available. The PRO is now seeking to make the local and national indexes uniform, based on the PRO film number plus the folio number stamped on the corner of alternate frames. It is not yet safe to assume that local index references will work at the PRO and vice-versa.

Quite a lot of the 1851 census has been indexed by Family History Societies. Some indexes give you the full name, age and birthplace, and the reference number. This is the PRO film number plus the 'folio' number, stamped on every other page of the enumeration books before they were filmed. Some just give a surname and reference. With the first kind, you may be able to tell right away if this is your family. With the others, you have to go to the original census, find and check every pair of pages with an instance of the surname, which is quite a chore if you have Smiths, Browns, Taylors etc. Still, if it is for a large city, it narrows down the field quite a lot. Most of the large conurbations, like Leeds, Manchester, Birmingham, Sheffield, Liverpool, Bristol, Nottingham, even London areas like City, Bethnal Green, Stepney, and Paddington are covered. The whole of Lincolnshire and Notts, almost all of Beds and substantial parts of other counties are completed (surnames only).

There are also some indexes for other census years: Nottinghamshire is very well served with surname/folio indexes to 1861 and 1881, and a private index of sections of London in 1871 has been started.

Most notable is the **1881 census index** compiled by volunteer family historians and processed by the Mormon church. It covers much of England and Wales and part of Scotland (1995) and is available through libraries, Mormon centres, and Family History Societies who participated in the work. This index lists each county alphabetically by surname, by birthplace, by location, and also provides a stylised form of the complete enumeration as it stands. It is not perfect, since original errors of enumerators have been retained rather than risk correction, and those from transcription and computer processing have been added. Because insufficient space was allocated, the occupation and address may be truncated, but it is a splendid tool which can help locate a missing family with limited clues to their whereabouts.

A detailed list of census indexes, with prices and addresses, is published as a Gibson Guide and new ones are being added all the time. You can purchase published indexes from the Family History Society concerned, though a few hold an index which can be consulted for a fee, and often a full transcript of any relevant entries can be supplied, which is useful if you cannot get to see the film. The local FHS will have full details as they are issued. The Census Search Room at the Public Record Office has copies of most of the published indexes.

The Census Index Room at the PRO has on shelves copies of most published indexes, also maps, particularly useful for cities, copies of some directories, and of the IGI, for locating possible parishes to search.

Obtaining a film

When you have the piece numbers of census entries you want to consult, go into the film reader rooms, and find your seat. Take the black card box with the number on it and go to the cabinets of films which line the walls, all labelled with the census year. Extract one numbered film from the cabinet, and put your black box in its place.

Films may be grouped together or sometimes one is split between two reels – it helps to note from the indexes if your place was at the beginning or end of the set of parishes listed for that piece number. It helps too if you memorise the couple of places before and after 'your' village – then you know when you are getting warm.

Missing censuses

A few sections of the census enumeration books went missing years back. If this happened, it is noted in the indexes. More difficult to track down is where a single page vanished before filming. At beginning or end, it may not be such a loss – just the formal pages – but if you find that part of a street is missing, check whether the actual page numbers (on each frame) run consecutively. If they don't, but the folio numbers on alternate pages do so run, then a sheet was either not filmed or lost before filming. You might ask to see the originals, if the Census Officer agrees (see page 72), but this is slow and usually unproductive. Usually, that part of the street is in another place, possibly unindexed because it isn't listed at the beginning of the enumeration book. You will have to hunt for it, using the help of a map to locate adjacent streets.

When you are working on the census of a town of any size, it is very helpful to take along an A-to-Z map to help with the location of the street. Some of the town street names will have changed since 1841–81, and some streets have vanished under main roads, but enough will remain for you to work out where the family lived.

Street name changes in towns were quite frequent, especially in London. The PRO has an official book of street name changes (enquire at the desk) for London, which helps if the street you have for 1862 seems not to exist in 1861.

Using a microfilm reader

If you have never threaded up a microfilm reader, but have used a film projector, you will find it simple enough. There are instructions on the photocopy table. What should happen is that the reel you are given goes on the left-hand spindle of the machine, with the keyhole slot facing and the film emerging from underneath. Feed this through the gate – the two small sheets of glass in the middle – under the empty spool and into the slot in the middle. Then shut the gate and wind away. Sometimes, people don't wind back their films from the right to the left hand reel when they finish, which means that you have to put the reel you are given on the right spindle and either wind back or work backwards. Sometimes they do worse things, like running the film from below on the left to above on the right, which puts the whole thing 'inside out', for the next reader. In this case, ask the person next to you for help, or go to an official.

If the whole film is upside-down, then turn the complete working head round on its swivel. If it is sideways – as the 1881 films are – turn the head half-way round. The focus can be adjusted by turning the knurled knob in the base of the machine at the front. Sometimes, this doesn't help enough, because the original book from which the film was made was badly written, or the writing has faded. This applies to 1841 especially. Try adjusting the focus knob or change the lens size. A smaller magnification may make a diffuse image clearer. A large one for a particular word may make sense of a pale or a scrawled word. You can concentrate the search on one place by easing the film spool by hand.

Reading the film

There may be two or three films on the same reel, so make sure you have the right one before starting your search. The film number is printed sideways at intervals through it, for example: 'HO 107 1234' or 'RG 10 321', as well as in large characters at the start of each one on the reel. Each piece is divided into *enumeration* books – sections of twenty or so pages – which may cover the whole of a tiny hamlet, part of a village or town, or a single section in a city. At the beginning of each book, the enumerator was supposed to enter the registration district, sub-district, the actual place, and the parish, if it was a town with multiple civil parishes, plus the district number he is dealing with (and pencilled on, there will be another figure, like a fraction, with the piece of number over the book number).

The enumerator was given a list of the streets or the area he had to cover, and this is normally set down on the front page of each book, which gives a quick reference to what it includes. After this come the printed pages, with instructions to the enumerator (these may be omitted from the film) and then the actual list of entries starts.

In 1841, the front pages were slightly less complicated, but contain similar information, with the book number written on, and the actual place covered at the end of the list of districts and sub-districts.

The entry pages show families grouped into households, as they come on the enumerator's walk round. Each household starts with the head of the family, and any non-members living in the same house are marked off by a single 'tick' on the left hand side, while the end of the household is marked by a double tick. In a town, you may get two or three households in the same house building. There are numbers in the far left-hand column, which are not street numbers, but merely the number of the household which is being enumerated. Street numbers were rare outside large towns (in the earlier censuses anyway) and where they occur, they come in the second column, which also gives the name of the road, in a town. In villages, in 1841, especially, there may be no street name at all – just 'village' or 'top end'.

Caveat: just because two households are next to each other in the enumerator's book, it does not follow they were immediate neighbours. On his first visit, the enumerator may not have found anyone at home, and have had to return later, initially omitting the household. The books themselves are fair copies, and a small household may have been inserted to fill up a page. This applies in later years as well.

Some of the names, ages, etc, will be scored through with large diagonal ticks. This doesn't mean they were wrong, but that the statistician had taken the information from the entry. Sometimes the occupations are 'corrected' so that they fit in with a class on his forms.

When you have found the village you seek, note down the reference data and year before you start – otherwise you can't make use of it or check back. Then take down every detail of the households where 'your' surname does occur. Even if they don't seem to belong at the moment, the names will probably fall into place later, and it is better to do a thorough search while you have the film out, rather than trek to the census room and go through the same hunt two or three times.

In a large town, there is less point in doing this with a common surname, but at least take those with the same birthplace as the ancestor, or the same occupation. If 'yours' have an uncommon Christian name in the family, then any other group with that Christian name might belong, even if the birthplace is different.

Reading difficulties

Most of the 1841 census is rather hard to read, because it was taken in pencil, and either that has rubbed or the paper has become grubby, or both, over the years, so the films are not very clear. Some later census enumerators economised on the ink, which has almost faded away, or wrote in a crabbed or semi-literate hand. The spelling in some cases is gallant rather than accurate. You may find that using a high magnification on a small area will help, or that a low magnification sharpens it up. There are alternate sizes on the PRO machines, changed by turning the section above the gate.

Some parts of the census (especially for 1841) were filmed on blue stock, which has deteriorated, and the image is so faint that no amount of juggling with the focus size will make it legible. If you get one of these ghosts of a film, it is sometimes possible to use the original books. Go to the Census Officer (desk next to the indexes) and say you have a 'blue film'. If he or she agrees that it is faulty, not just hard to read, you will be given a chitty to see the original. This will take a couple of days to produce, as it is not kept in London, but in the store room at Hayes, Middlesex.

There is nothing anyone can do about bad writing, faded ink, or damaged sheets. And it is up to you to locate and read the entry referring to your family. Sometimes the entry is there, but disguised by odd spelling – 'Horsebone' for Osborne, or 'Olding' for Holdham – so check carefully. Sometimes Grandpa did decide to move a couple of days before the census was taken. And if you find an address in a directory for a census year, remember it was normally compiled from the previous year's information.

Photocopies at the PRO

The Census Room has an excellent photocopy service, rapid and of high quality, which will sometimes improve a pale original, though not bad writing. When you find the entry you want copied, make a careful note of the full identifying reference to it. That is the year code and piece number (from the side of the film) plus information to locate the exact page.

For 1841, this is the Book Number – at the beginning of each schedule enumerated – plus the folio number, on the top right-hand corner of the page, and the page

     eg HO 107/44   bk 2   folio 5.   page 14

From 1851 onwards, give the year code and piece number plus the folio number, which is the big one at the top of every other page, and which covers the next page too (add 'b' if you like for the reverse side) plus the smaller page number, which appears on every side, either in the centre, or right, at the top. If you want a whole set of folios, running consecutively, then state the first and last folio/page numbers and the total number of single sheets (frames). The current cost is 70p a frame.

When you have a reference, wind back the film and take it to the photocopy section, near the Indexes, where you can take a copy for a small fee.

Using local copies

These are now widespread (see page 108) and may be easier to get at and use. Some places have their own set of reference numbers, but if you are doing this seriously, take a note of the PRO reference too (from the side of the film). Then if you ever want to exchange information with someone else at a distance, your reference will mean something. The same applies if one day you intend to publish a family history.

Local libraries and record offices may use different types of microfilm readers, which are threaded in a manner other than that described above. Reader-printers, for instance, are often threaded from top to top of the spools – so *ask* the first time you use them.

Reader-printers produce quick and convenient photocopies – you merely locate your entry and press the button, without winding off and on. These copies cost, typically, 15p or 20p.

What is the census?

This is most easily illustrated by using a fictitious but typical example. The village of Sprotley in Loamshire is being searched, because family tradition says that the ancestor, James Bloggs, was born here, and in about 1840, according to his age at death. He does not appear, but there are Bloggses in the village, so all instances of the surname are noted and also all other mentions of the names Allen, Porter and Starkey, which happen to occur in Bloggs households. Spelling varies, but this is immaterial, at a time when not everyone could write and fewer still were confident about spelling even their own name.

Interpretation

As no relationships are given, we can only guess. *Household 14* is probably that of a husband and wife, William and Mary. The younger folk could all be their children. The 2 year old, William, could be a son of Mary (aged 40–45) or her grandson. Ann Porter might be her mother, William's widowed mother remarried, some other poor relation or just a lodger. James Allan, the Scottish-born man of independent means, is doubtful. He could be a lodger or an overnight visitor. *Household 23* could be a widower, Henry (40–45) and his children from oldest to youngest. The intervention of Anne Starkey in the middle of the family casts doubts on this. Perhaps she and the younger children are the grandchildren of Henry.

Example:

1841 Census for SPROTLEY Loamshire. HO 107 125 bk. 3.

'All that part of the parish of Sprotley north of the turnpike by Gatley's Mill and the Honble Mr Dennysons.'

PLACE	HOUSES		NAMES of each Person who abode therein the preceding night	Age and Sex		PROFESSION, TRADE, EMPLOYMENT or of INDEPENDENT MEANS	WHERE BORN	
	(A)	(B)*		Males	Females		(C)	(D)*
(folio 4) Village								
No. 14		x	William Bloggs	42		shepherd	Y	
			Mary Bloggs		40		N	
			John Bloggs	25		shepherd	N	
			Sarah Bloggs		20		N	
			Jane Bloggs		15		N	
			Mary Bloggs		12		Y	
			George Bloggs	10			Y	
			William Bloggs	2			N	
			Anne Porter		70	pauper	Y	
			James Allan	70		Ind	N	S
(folio 5)								
No. 23		x	Henery Bloggs	45		ag lab	Y	
			Sarah Bloggs		25		Y	
			Joseph Bloggs	20			Y	
			John Bloggs	15			Y	
			Ann Starkey		5		N	
			Peter Bloggs	3			Y	
			Jane Bloggs		8 mo		Y	
No. 26		x	William Dokes	35		ag lab	Y	
			Mary Dokes		30		Y	
			William Porter	45		carter	N	
(folio 10)								
No. 46		x	Caleb Grimes	60		gardener	N	
[next door			Thirza Grimes		65		N	
to Manor,			Matilda Truscott		30	sempstress	N	
Mr Dennison]			Andrew Allen	40		gardener	N	
			Robert Allen	35		gardener	N	
			Sarah Bloggs		12	F S	Y	

*Column sub-headings: *(A) Uninhabited or building: (B) Inhabited; (C) Whether Born in same County; (D) Whether Born in Scotland, Ireland or Foreign Parts.*

Other abbreviations:

Y = born in county; N = Not born in county; S = born in Scotland; I = born in Ireland; F P = born in foreign parts; Ag Lab = agricultural labourer; Ind = of independent means; Annt = Annuitant; F S = female servant; M S = male servant; do. = ditto.

Other abbreviations for occupations which appear regularly may be used, some local: FWK = framework knitter (Notts., Leics.); C M = coal miner (Wales); W M = watch maker (St Helens area); chairmr = chairmaker (Bucks.); HLW = hand loom weaver (cotton areas).

The Porter in *Household 26* might belong, but it is a common name and might be irrelevant anyway – but well . . . *Household 46* was noted because two surnames found in the major Bloggs household also occur here. Probably the Grimes pair are husband and wife – though they could be brother and sister. The two Allens in the same household may be brothers – relatives often worked together on large estates. Matilda Truscott may be a relative or a visiting dressmaker – though temporary visitors generally come last in the household, except for servants. Sarah Bloggs, the little servant girl, may be related to one of the other families found, or an incomer.

The proportion of persons not born in the county is higher than normal, in this extracted group, but may be accounted for by the fact that Sprotley is a border village. The 'Noes' may have been born a mile or so away.

The fact that there is no sign of James Bloggs born *c.*1840 isn't conclusive. Ages at death are notoriously unreliable, because the person who knew is in no position to say. The census refers to the situation on one night only – so if your ancestor is away from home then, he won't appear, even if he did live in the place for the other 364 days of the year.

Having found that the family surname occurs is a good reason for searching later censuses. Even if they hadn't been there, a strong family tradition would be a good reason to search further.

It is impossible to make an accurate family tree from the 1841 census alone, because no relationships are stated. However, it is always worthwhile extracting information from that census, since it catches the families at an early stage, and the relationships can be checked from later censuses and other records.

The 1851 census and later ones

The extra information in these censuses, in particular the birthplaces and family relationships, will enable you to build up a family tree, to be checked and amplified from other sources.

In the Sprotley extracts shown here, the family begins to shape up, and some of its past and present history can be established.

Interpretation

The 1851 data confirms that William and Mary Bloggs are husband and wife. Their ages in 1841 were 48 and 44, correctly rounded down to 45 and 40. William was born in the next parish east and Mary in the next west – which happens to be over the county boundary. Their daughter Jane, aged 16 ('15') at the last census, has married well, to a tradesman, and is now visiting home, with her children. Mary, whose age varies slightly between censuses, has been a servant, but is now unemployed. Lady Day (March 25) was a usual day to change jobs. Unemployment was rare for a good maid from a decent family, so maybe she was ill, or her mother was, or possibly she was just about to marry. Or maybe she was going to have a baby – accidents will happen even in the best homes.

Although Ann Porter has presumably died, her probable status as Mary's mother is confirmed by the presence in the household of the disabled brother-in-law. The parish registers of Newchurch should confirm this rapidly.

Household 38.   John and Sarah Bloggs are revealed as husband and wife, not brother and sister. They were probably staying with Mother for the birth of the new baby then imminent. The 1841 census was taken in early June, the 1851 in late March – and James could be 9 and almost 10 months, which fits in with the structure of the family, including 8 year old Margaret, staying with grandpa Allan. In the house is an unknown sister, acting as nurse-housekeeper for the first month from birth. There

Example: CENSUS 1851. HO 107 1345 sch. 4a (folios 92–119) LOAMSHIRE.
Supt. Reg. District OLDCHURCH, sub-district SPROTLEY.

'Sprotley – all that part of the village north of the turnpike including Low Meadow, Hartleys, Dark Lane, Mill Way, the Mill, Hoggins Farm, Budds Cottages and Mr Dennison's Park.'

The first two columns are headed *No. of Householder's Schedule* and *Names of Street, Place or Road, and Name or No. of House;* the final column is headed *Whether Blind, or Deaf and Dumb.* Cdn. = Condition, ie Married, Single, Widowed; *M* = Male; *F* = Female.

Name and surname of each person who abode in the house, on the Night of 30th March	Relation to head of Family	Cdn.	Age of M	Age of F	Rank, Profession or Occupation	Where Born
24. Dark Lane						
William Bloggs	head	marr	58		shepherd	Loamshire, Peasley
Mary Bloggs	wife	marr		54	shepherd's wife	Clayshire, Newchurch
Mary Bloggs	dau	unm		23	servant out of place	Loams., Sprotley
Jane Johnson	dau visitor	marr		26	wife of butcher	Clays., Weston
Mary Johnson	grdau visitor	unm		4	scholar	Loams., Morton
James Johnson	grson visitor	unm	2		scholar	Loams., Morton
William Porter	bro in law	unm	57		pauper	Clays., Newchurch
[in final column: 'blind and lame by a cart haveing passed over him']						
38. Mill Way						
John Bloggs	head	marr	35		shepherd	Clays., Newchurch
Sarah Bloggs	wife	marr		33	lacemaker	Clays., Newchurch
William Bloggs	son	unm	12		asst shepherd	Loams., Copton
James Allan Bloggs	son	unm	9		scholer	Loams., Sprotley
Mary Ann Bloggs	dau	unm		6	scholer	Loams., Sprotley
Jane Bloggs	dau	unm		4	scholer	Loams., Sprotley
Sarah Ann Bloggs	dau	unm		2	at home	Loams., Sprotley
Harriot Bloggs	dau	unm		2 weeks		Loams., Sprotley
Ann Griffin	sister	widow		32	monthly nurse	Clays., Weston
47. Mill Way						
James Allan	head	widr	81		annuitant, fmr gardner	Scotld, Perth, Ochrarader
Margaret Bloggs	grdau	unm		8	scholar	Loams., Sprotley
Elizabeth Tibbets	servt	wid		62	housekeeper	Clays., Newchurch
54. Budds Cottages						
Henry Bloggs	head	marr	55		ag lab	Loams., Peasley
Sarah Bloggs	wife	marr		39	lacemaker	Loams., Sprotley
Anna Starkey	dau in law	unm		15	lacemaker	Clays., Weston
Peter Bloggs	son	unm	12		carter's boy	Loams., Sprotley
Jane Bloggs	dau	unm		11	lacemaker	Loams., Sprotley
Henry Bloggs	son	unm	8		lame from birth	Loams., Sprotley
James Bloggs	son	unm	4		scholer	Loams., Sprotley
Hannah Bloggs	dau	unm		1	scholer	Loams., Sprotley
55. Budds Cottages						
Joseph Bloggs	head	marr	32		ag lab	Loams., Sprotley
Hannah Bloggs	wife	marr		38	landress	Loams., Copton
Betsy Bloggs	dau	unm		7	asst landress	Loams., Sprotley
Peter Bloggs	son	unm	6 mo			Loams., Sprotley
Sara Gates	sister	widow		22	sempstress	Loams., Morton
68. Mr Dennison's Cottage, Park						
Andrew Allan	head	marr	51		head gardner	Clays., Newchurch
Matilda Allan	wife	marr		43	dressmaker	Clays., Newchurch
James Thomas Allan	son	unm	5		scholar	Loams., Sprotley
Robert Allan	brother	unm	48		asst gardner	Clays., Newchurch deaf for 40 years

were many young widows, since what are now minor infections so often proved fatal then. Unless they remarried rapidly, the only respectable skills were nursing and dressmaking. John, like father, is a shepherd, one of the most skilled jobs in agriculture, so comparatively well-paid.

Household 47. James Allan, the last member of the Bloggs household in 1841, is revealed as Sarah's father. His former occupation was as gardener and educated guesswork suggests that he was formerly Mr Dennison's head gardener at the Manor. There was a fashion for Scots gardeners in the nineteenth century – and only a wealthy man could afford to give annuities to old employees. This could be checked in the will of old Mr Dennison (the current one is only 38). The birthplace, though mis-spelled, is recognisable. This is a bonus – many Scots and Irish just state the country or at best their county of birth. We can guess that Margaret was the name of James Allan's wife, since it was rare outside Scotland and the north of England, till later in the century.

Household 66. Although proof can only come from the parish registers of Newchurch, it seems likely that Andrew and Robert Allan are James's sons, following his trade. Matilda Truscott of 1841 may be the widowed daughter or niece of the Grimeses, and when they died or retired, the apparently confirmed bachelor married her, for convenience and propriety.

Household 54. Sarah is shown to be the second wife, not the daughter, of Henry. She was either a young widow or had an illegitimate daughter, Anna Starkey, which would make her vulnerable to an older man. The precise size of the first family of Henry is uncertain. There may be more than Joseph, John and Sarah.

It seems likely that William and Henry Bloggs are brothers (or cousins) which can be checked in the Peasley registers. Although it may seem unnecessary at first sight to study Henry's family in depth, it all belongs. Uncles and cousins are part of family history and often have great influence. The presence of James in the family, born 1846/7, could be important. Your James was not known as James Allan later – could the age be badly wrong at death? If there is another marriage for James Allan, plain James could be yours. All alternatives should be studied at first, and eliminated, or you may find yourself spending months barking up the wrong fmaily tree, or the wrong branch of it.

Some people are very tempted to pick the more 'desirable' alternatives, rejecting bastards or paupers, which is silly. Ancestors who have made it from poor beginnings are worthwhile people, after all.

Of course, not all families will stay tidily in one place and provide so much confirmatory data in just two censuses, but over the five available, a useful chunk of family tree will emerge, at least in rural areas, which can then be checked against official dates of registration in St Catherine's House.

The important thing is that many persons born before 1837 appear in the censuses – pre-registration. Sometimes there are people still alive in 1851 who were born far back into the eighteenth century, and their birthplaces are stated, which will lead you back to the appropriate parish or chapel registers.

Even for town ancestors, censuses are vital sources, since the nineteenth century was a great period of transfer from country to town. If the surname you are researching is a common one, the census may provide the only clue to *which* George Brown, among the many registered at St Catherine's, is yours. The presence of in-laws in the household may obviate the need for buying expensive certificates of marriage, and even with second generation townies, country cousins may be there on a visit. The wealthier families often got their servants from 'back home' too.

Information from later censuses

It is possible to obtain very limited information from the 1901 census, though this is a desperation course to take only if your ancestor had eluded every previous census and you have a positive address for that year. You cannot see the census itself, but if you write to OPCSS, St Catherine's House, 10 Kingsway, London, WC2 6JP, you will be sent a form. You must be (or have written permission from) a direct descendant and state that the information is for family history purposes, not litigation. It will cost around £20 and the only information given is the age and birthplace for named persons at the exact address. If they happen to be away working or visiting on census night, well hard luck. You won't normally get the family either. It is not proposed to open the 1911 census in this way, because of procedural problems. The Scottish 1901 census is similarly available from GRO, New Register House, Edinburgh EH1 3YT. The Irish 1901 and 1911 censuses are open, replacing earlier lost censuses.

Censuses before 1841

Censuses were taken every ten years from 1801. All the government required was a count of heads, with the population broken down by age and sex. The counts were taken by local men – often the schoolmaster or curate – and, obviously, the best way to do it was to make a list of local householders by name and note their dependents in the various ages – sometimes by name too. The 'five year banding' system was used, whereby all children in the household between 5 and 10, or all adults from 25 to 30, were grouped and counted. The totals in each group were then sent in to the government and the original notes usually destroyed.

Just a few were kept by chance, and others were not only kept but amplified with extra notes about the occupations and even places of origin. This only happened if the enumerator was keen on local history and had time to indulge his curiosity.

There were many other unofficial local listings of population which are similar to censuses, made for various reasons at earlier times. These may be all householders, all males, poor people, ratepayers, etc. Many of these are included in *Local Census Listings* (Gibson) and *Pre-1841 Census Listings* (C Chapman).

Scotland and Ireland

Scottish censuses are kept at the General Register Office, New Register House, Edinburgh EH1 3YT (where the indexes to births, marriages and deaths since 1858 are found). This is in West Register Street, off Princes Street, opposite the North British Hotel. You have to pay for access – £5 a day to see the censuses alone, or £11 for access to registers of birth, marriage and death and older parish registers as well. If you plan a full day's work, rather than popping in for half an hour, you will get value. If you want to make a longer search in all these records, you have to pay a daily or weekly fee for access. This is more economic if combined with a general search.

By post, the staff will search a census film if you supply exact enough information of place and family required and supply a certified copy for a fee. If they can't find the entry – and they are very conscientious – they return half the fee. For single entries where you know the location and some names, this is much cheaper than using a searcher, but not for multiple entries where your information is vague. If you do the work yourself, you can copy down the entries or get a half-price certified copy while your day pass is valid.

Irish censuses of the nineteenth century are, for all practical purposes, non-existent. There are bits left, but never the bits you want. Check with the Irish Public Record Office, Four Courts, Dublin 1, to see if you are among the fortunate few. The 1901 and 1911 censuses are open to inspection, though these normally state only the county for birthplace. They do, however, give extra information, like religious denomination, number of rooms in the house, and it is possible to assemble a fair idea of the house from the details given. These censuses may be available through LDS Family History Centres.

SOMERSET HOUSE WILLS FROM 1858

The route we have followed so far is the main stream of research, through official records which apply to everyone. There are a few side channels which could help to forward the research.

A boost from directories

Directories, for locating addresses in census years, I have already mentioned. If you do find your ancestors there, then you can check for an entry in every available year, which will tell you when your ancestor started up in business, and when he ceased. Remember that directories are usually compiled the year before, then printed, so someone in the 1892 edition could have died in January 1892, or even December 1891.

Sometimes there are even display adverts, which tell you just what the ancestor sold, and that he was doing pretty well at it. If the ad states that James sells 'our Patent Hanging Lamp' you could at some stage go to the Patents Office in Silver Court, off Chancery Lane in London, and actually see the drawings and description of the lamp. And if you frequent antique or junk shops, who knows, you might even find such a lamp. If you remember not to shout with joy, and alert the shop owner to your special interest, you might even be able to afford it, too.

Look out for other persons of the same name in the same trade, who could be relatives. Before James Bloggs is listed, was there another? If not, who was running a business from the same address, and did James marry his daughter?

Men of property

People who lived in houses were responsible for paying various rates based on their value. Payment of rates was generally recorded, and at least in towns, these records should have survived, perhaps still in a town hall, perhaps in the CRO or library. Sometimes the landlord paid, but often enough the tenant – and this is a way of finding out addresses for people who don't quite make directories. The rate books can also show when Mr Jardine dies and Mrs Jardine takes over, or who was living at the unexpected address where Great-Uncle Fred died – could be a married daughter.

There are also Electoral registers, which in the early days can be very limited, showing only those who were qualified to vote by owning or tenanting large enough properties. More townspeople qualified, with 'householder' votes, and then up-market lodger votes and finally votes for all males over 21. Women over 30 got the vote in 1919 and over 21 in 1928. So on the whole, you would be able to locate men in towns, but not families, until sixty years back. It could be useful for the period after the 1881 census.

The earlier registers do show people who own land in one place but live in another – very useful for tracing movements and proving particular families are linked. Before 1872, printed Poll Books show you not only who could vote, but how they voted, before the secret ballot.

Did they leave wills?

Unless your ancestors were determinedly poor always, there should be at least a few wills in the family. Even if your own lot were poor, there could well be aunties with a bit tucked away, or richer relations, who did leave wills. In the case of the Bloggs family, they were tradesmen, which means someone paid for their apprenticeships, and they themselves were better paid than labourers, so it is very much worth trying.

Wills fall into two classes – those before 1858, proved in the ecclesiastical courts and now mainly found in the area where they were made; and wills proved from early January 1858, which may include some made well before that date. All these later wills for England and Wales are to be found in the Principal Probate Registry at Somerset House in London, and a visit there is likely to be a rewarding experience.

You can trace the wills of ancestors whose death dates you know, and see them on the spot, which could give you a complete list of the children, grandchildren, in-laws, cousins etc. You can also work through the indexes, which are very detailed, and pick out whole groups of 'family'. Often this can give you a fresh lead to further research, if you spot a known name as 'nephew and executor' to an unknown's will. The addresses in the indexes could point the way to a census search too. And a good family will may contain comments on the character and habits of your kinsfolk. In fact, wills are one of the most useful tools for family historians.

Somerset House: the indexes

Since January 1858, all wills have been proved in civil courts – either the Principal Probate Registry in London, or the offices of the District Probate Registries in various parts of the country. Wherever they were proved in England or Wales, the indexes have been combined centrally, and can be seen freely at Somerset House in the Strand, London. These annual indexes were printed, and sets are available at provincial centres, page 94.

The Principal Probate Registry (now called the Principal Registry of the Family Division) in the Strand is at the back of the hollow square of buildings which form Somerset House and access is through the gateway from the Strand and across the car park (not intended for public use). Anyone can go there, between the hours of 10 am and 4.30 pm, from Mondays to Fridays, and look at the indexes of wills for nothing and actually see copies of the wills themselves, from all over England and Wales, for a small fee.

The *indexes* have the names of testators, filed in alphabetical order, according to the date when the will was proved, which may be a while after the person died. For every year from 1858 until about nine months from the current date, these indexes are all available, mostly in bound sets, with all the names in their alphabetical order. *Letters of Administration* (abbreviation: Admons.) might be issued if a person left no will. These Administrations are indexed in the same books, before 1870 following the wills, since then mixed in with them, always clearly indicated in the books themselves. The latest indexes are available in a computerised form, which is by no means simple to use.

The index entry in itself contains a great deal of valuable information. For a will, this may include the name of the deceased; possibly his occupation; his address when the will was made and any other address where a later codicil was made; the precise date and place of death; very occasionally the cause of death (eg a street accident); the date and court of the probate; the name(s) of the executor(s), the address, either occupation or relationship to the deceased, if stated in the will; if there are or were other executors named in the will; the amount of the estate sworn; and revisions of the figure made later; the date of any later grant (eg if an executor dies before completing his work).

An Administration where there is a will but, for various reasons, no executor, shows the same details. An administration for a person who has made no will (see *Intestacy*) has the name and address of the deceased, the date of death, the date and place of the grant and the name of the administrator, who is normally the next of kin.

Seeing the will

Where there is a will, it is almost always worth having a look at it. The exception is where the executor (or administrator) is described as 'universal legatee', since all the will says is 'all I possess to my dear wife Maggie'. Otherwise, when you have found the entry in the index, take the whole book to the counter on the left, where you will be asked if you want to see the will. Resist the temptation to be facetious – the alternative is to order a photocopy, sight unseen, which is what the lads from the lawyers' offices do. It costs more, it is slower, but the client pays, so who cares.

The official will write the name and reference on a ticket – if there are two entries of the same name in the same year, make sure you point to the correct one upside-down. Then take the ticket along the corridor on the right to the Cashier's Office and pay 25p. Take the ticket back to the counter, and the official will hand it over to the porters.

While you take the index book back to its shelf – not forgetting to copy out the details first – the will copy or register is being found in the miles of shelving in the store. A London (Principal Probate Registry) will is located within ten minutes or less, but a 'country will' is stored further away and may take up to half an hour to be produced on a busy day. Each time the lift in the corner whines up, listen to the porters, who call out, not YOUR name, but the name on the will. Signal when you hear it, and they put the will on a table for you to read, either opening the book or marking the place with a tag. These books are dirty, so don't go dressed in your best.

You can then read the will, or make an abstract from it, but not copy it down word for word. This senseless restriction doesn't matter, for once, because wills are full of legal gobbledegook and repetitions, which can be reduced considerably in volume. Make an abstract of the important bits, which are basically the names, addresses, relationships, details of legacies and any personal comments or special phrases which will illuminate the family history.

The older wills were copied in a large round handwriting, with occasional fancy twiddles, but with a bit of concentration, these can be mastered. The copy has to be exact, so if the testator wrote it himself, you may get the full flavour of Grandpa's mis-spellings and odd phraseology. If you doubt your ability or are running out of time, or just fancy the will for display, you can get a copy of the whole or part of it after all, for about 25p a page. Since some wills run to a dozen pages, making an abstract is cheaper and much quicker, and not nearly as difficult as it seems. A tremendous lot of the verbiage will be standard phrases, which you can discard, and the rest can be translated into a short form (see page 91).

What is a will?

A will makes provision for the disposal of real and personal estate belonging to the TESTATOR or TESTATRIX. Real estate is freehold houses, land (and peerage titles, where this applies). Personal estate is leasehold houses and land, stocks and shares, insurances, household goods, stock in trade, tools and implements, cash, debts owing, jewellery, etc, etc. All these possessions are to be shared out, usually among family and friends, in amounts or percentages laid down by the testator. This task is performed by the EXECUTOR, executrix or executors appointed in the will, after he or she or they have obtained the right to do so by proving the will in the Probate Court.

LEGACIES – the money or property left by the testator – may dispose of property **absolutely**, with no strings attached, or **conditionally**, with certain limitations. The most common limitation is a **life interest** or **life rent**, whereby the legatee (a widow or son, say) has the use of or income from the particular property for life, after which it passes to another named person. The person with the life interest cannot sell or otherwise dispose of the property and it is normally in the control of trustees (probably the same as the executors). A widow might lose her life interest in her husband's estate if she remarried or have the legacy greatly reduced. A legacy to a daughter might be withheld if she married without consent, or 'during couverture' (while married) or while a particular husband lived. This was influenced by the law concerning married women's property (see page 87).

A will normally disposes of real estate first, then leaseholds, then business premises and equipment, then personal effects, then money. On the whole, provision was first made for the widow, who might be left the family home, or a smaller house, or an annuity bought from the estate or payable out of income from rents or a business, plus household furniture and effects. She might have these for life or until she remarried. Only legacies left 'absolutely' or 'at her own dispose' really belonged to her properly.

The children were dealt with next. The eldest son would expect to inherit most of the real estate and the family business, while his brothers would get subsidiary property or money to set them up in life. If, for any reason, the testator mistrusted the abilities of a particular son, he might leave him a life interest only, with remainder to a named brother or grandson, but he could not tie the hands of his heirs in perpetuity, only those then alive. Daughters were generally given a dowry when they married. Unmarried girls were expected to stay with Mother, though if they were 'on the shelf' already, Father might make generous provision for their old age, since no jobs would be open to them. Sons may be listed before daughters in a will, but if a mixed list is given, it is likely to be in order of age.

Bequests to remoter relatives and friends come next and these are often useful in adding to the family tree. Wills of spinsters and widows are particularly full of cousins and side branches of the family. It is never a waste of time to note down the details of these minor bequests for, at the very least, they give an idea of the style and standard of living and the personal interests of the testator.

The will ends with a standard attestation clause to show that the testator has formally adopted the document as his will and signed it in the presence of two witnesses. A blind or illiterate person can make a legal will, which is then read over to him before witnesses, and signed for him. If he puts his finger on the will (on the seal if any) and accepts it, it is legal. The witness should not be a beneficiary or the spouse of one. If such a person signs, the will is legal but the legacy is forfeit. From this section of the will, you will need only the date and signature, and any unusual circumstances, as above. The witnesses' names should be noted.

It is normal to include a clause leaving the residue of the estate to named persons. Even when the testator knows what he has to leave, this is advisable, since he could acquire more property or a legacy might lapse (see page 87). If the appointed executor cannot or will not act, the residuary legatee most closely related to the executor is made administrator.

If the testator changes his mind after making the will, he can write a new one. Then he must destroy the old one, not just scribble on it, and say in the new one that he revokes all past wills. If he wants to keep most of the will but to revoke one legacy – to an erring son – or to add a bequest to a new infant, he can add a *codicil* dealing with this, which is proved with the original will. Care has to be taken that it does not contradict the will nor leave the same property twice, so that it often takes a great many words to say what it means. The codicil must be signed and witnessed and attested like the will itself.

An executor or executors should be appointed by the testator to carry out the provisions of the will. His/their first duty is to arrange the funeral and provide for any emergency measures which must be taken in connection with the family or business of the deceased. He must then prepare a list of the property of the deceased with its value – on which estate duty is levied – and take or have a solicitor take the will to probate. Of recent years, it has become a custom to appoint a firm of solicitors or bank as executor, or joint executor, but formerly it was more usual for a relative to act – a widow or adult son – or a trusted business associate.

Once probate has been granted, the executor takes possession of the estate (from the Probate Judge, who has technically owned it since the death of the testator). He pays the debts – and gets in what is owing – hands over specific legacies, and sells whatever he has been instructed to sell, and transfers any property bequeathed to the legatee. The remaining estate is then distributed in sums or shares as ordered and the final account is made. This is the end of the task, if all the legacies are given absolutely.

If certain legacies were conditional, the executor's task may continue for years, and he will normally be appointed as *trustee*, since he is 'on trust' to fulfil the rest of the will. If money is to be invested and the income paid to named persons, then there are strict rules about the type of stock in which investments may be made. Trustees are normally empowered to take their expenses from the estate, and absolved from any losses caused accidentally or otherwise than by malpractice. If a trustee dies, others may be appointed. All this is detailed at great length and all you need to note is 'standard trustee clauses'.

Administration plus will; Limitations; Scotland

Executors can refuse to take on the burden, or, having taken it on, they may resign or die before getting very far with the tasks involved. In that case, or where the testator fails to name an executor at all, an administrator is appointed by the court. This will normally be the residuary legatee who is next of kin to the deceased and able to act. If there is no residuary legatee, then the ordinary next of kin is appointed, or the principal legatee under the will. If the next of kin or residuary legatee is a minor, then the guardian can act. An administrator may be appointed if the executor named is abroad, goes mad, cannot cope with a legal dispute, etc. In all these cases, there will be a will. For administration without a will, see *Intestacy*.

Wills are automatically revoked by marriage or remarriage, in England and Wales, unless they were made just before the wedding and 'in contemplation of marriage', like the older marriage settlements. In Scotland, marriage does not revoke a will, but the birth of a child to the testator does. In England, the birth does not revoke a will and the father must make a codicil to include it, unless his will refers to 'all my children' already. Scottish wills need not be signed by the testator in the presence of his witnesses, provided he tells them it is his will.

English law allows a person to dispose of his whole estate at whim, provided he is adult, sane, solvent and male. There were limitations on married women born and married before 1883 (see *Married Women's Property*). Idiots, persons of unsound mind at the time of making the will, persons suffering brain damage, etc, cannot make a legal will, neither can minors (under 21 until the age of majority became 18), except for minor members of the armed forces in war or mariners in peril.

Bankrupts or persons heavily in debt cannot will away property to which their creditors are entitled, and debts will be a first charge on the estate, before any share-out is made. In fact, the heir of a bankrupt will be at least morally obliged to make good any deficit, especially if pre-death gifts were made to him after the testator's estate got rocky.

In Scotland, a married man with children may not dispose freely of his own estate. One third must go to the widow, one third to the children and only the last third – 'the deid's part' – may be left at whim. If there is a widow but no children, or children alone, then the reserved part is a half and the dead's part the other half. Minors may make legal wills in Scotland, though formerly only to dispose of personal estate. Most Scottish wills proved centrally or locally may be seen at the Scottish Record Office, Register House, Edinburgh, though some are retained by local Sheriff Courts.

Lapsed legacies

The fact that a person was left something in a will does not prove that he got it. If a specific item – a house, a painting – was bequeathed, but sold before the testator died, the legacy lapsed. So did it if the legatee died before the testator, unless they died at the same time exactly, and then the older is deemed to have died first. If the legatee was child of the testator, by a legal fiction he or she was deemed to have died afterwards, even if the fact was that he/she died some years before. This meant that, if the son or daughter left children, they would inherit the legacy which would have come to their parent, sharing it (*per stirpes*).

Legacies are normally paid to minors only when they become 21 or marry and a testator can set 25 or later as the age for payment if he fancies doing so. If the legatee dies before reaching this age, then the legacy lapses, but it was usual to allow for this by leaving the *Remainder* to the child or children of the deceased legatee. Where a legacy was left to a group of people, as, for instance, the children of a particular brother or sister, one or more of whom might die before getting their share, it could be arranged that the lapsed share went to all the others in the group in equal parts. The process was known as *benefit of survivorship* and several lines of the will explaining this can be reduced to 'ben.surv.'

Married women's property

Until 1883, the ordinary married woman had no property of her own, even the clothes she stood up in. 'Husband and wife are one person, and that person is the husband' was the legal position. A wife could therefore not make a will. In certain circumstances, a father or other relative might leave a specific sum to the wife, with instructions that she should be allowed to dispose of it at death by 'a writing or deed' and these deeds of gift are proved like wills, but the system relied heavily on the co-operation of the husband, who could spend the money first. From 1883 onwards married women were allowed to dispose of money they owned at marriage or acquired in their own right after that date, but this did not apply to women married before 1883 retrospectively, and they could only deal with what they acquired after that date, not the dowry they had on marriage, unless a super-indulgent husband allowed them to do so.

Cautious fathers and uncles, before and for some time after 1883, continued to leave property intended for married daughters to trustees, who were instructed to pay the income only to the wife, and sometimes specifying 'free from any debts or incumbrances of her present or any other husband' and allowing her to have the principal only when widowed, or not at all, and giving the 'remainder' to her children when of age.

This type of clause does not necessarily indicate that Father disliked the son-in-law, only the system, but if the trustees are instructed to pay the money 'as and when convenient' and the husband is 'not to inter-meddle' with the arrangements, this may mean that Father suspects The Worst.

Warning

The existence of a legacy is no proof that it was paid to the person named, even if he/she survived the testator, and to the age laid down in a condition. Always add up the legacies and see if the total matches up to the estate. A man might dispose of property or lose his money after making his will and before dying. The executor had to pay for the funeral, the probate charges and then the debts. If the remaining estate was insufficient, real estate had to be sold to pay this and meet demands of the creditors. Only then would specific legacies be paid, and the residue, if any, divided. If the estate was not sufficient to meet all legacies, then they would, by agreement, be settled *pro rata*. There might be no residue left to share after that, to the loss of close family members.

Intestacy

If a man died without making a will, his estate was divided between his relatives according to certain rules, which have varied over the years. You can check the exact position most easily in an edition of *Whitaker's Almanack* for the appropriate year, which gives a simple summing up in comprehensible terms. Distribution depends on the number and close-ness of surviving relatives.

Before 1926, real estate was treated separately from personal estate. If a man left a widow and children, the widow got a life interest in a third of the real estate and the eldest son the rest. If there were children only, the eldest son took the lot. If he had died before, leaving heirs, his son (or sons in succession) inherited. If he left daughters, they shared equally. If the line of the eldest son failed, then the next brother and his heirs inherited, and so on. A childless wife got her third and the husband's father, or his brothers in turn, their heirs, sisters sharing, grandparents, uncles and aunts and their heirs could take the rest, in sequence as above, with closer relatives always preferred to distant ones, and males of any group to females. If there were no relatives, the widow got her third for life and the Crown took the rest.

Personal estate, which included leaseholds, together with real estate after 1926, was placed in the hands of an administrator and turned into money, which was then distributed to relatives with a claim. A husband took the lot until recently and a widow would get the whole of a 'small estate' only. 'Small' was set at different levels at different dates. In 1890, the amount was £500, in 1926 it was £1,000 and 'personal chattels'; of recent years, the 'small estate' increased to £15,000 and personal effects. Everything above that amount was shared according to the amount and relationship of family left by the deceased.

In 1890, the widow got a third, the children two-thirds. From 1926, the widow got a life interest in half the residue, the children the rest. Nowadays, the childless widow gets £40,000 before division. In 1890, if there were no other relatives than the widow, the Crown took half the estate, now the widow gets it all, just as a man would have done anyway. If there are no blood relatives within the prescribed degrees (that is, sharing common grandparents) the State takes all.

Large sums advanced to relatives by the deceased and (before 1926) real estate inherited through him, had to be 'put into hotchpot' or included in the gross value of the estate and as part of that person's share. An illegitimate child had no automatic right of inheritance at all, and could not claim anything from his father, only from his mother. Nowadays an illegitimate child has a right of inheritance, but obviously has to prove paternity or show it was admitted in the father's lifetime.

Lapsed legacies which had not been remaindered, and the share of a residuary legatee who died first, if there was no benefit of survivorship clause, were treated as part of the estate, and distributed according to the laws of intestacy.

Administrators would be appointed by the Probate Court, and would normally be the next of kin, unless that person was a minor, absent from England, etc, a bankrupt, or incapable mentally. In the case of a minor, the natural guardian was made administrator (a grandfather or uncle, say), and the minor could take over and administer when he came of age, if all the assets had not then been distributed. If the testator was insolvent, the major creditor(s) might be appointed to wind up the estate, or a Probate Court official.

Despite the Englishman's general power to dispose of his estate at whim, cutting out his nearest and supposedly dearest, dependent persons could always claim maintenance from an estate of sufficient size. Dependents were widows; minor children, unmarried daughters of any age; sons of full age disabled mentally or physically; orphan grandchildren. More recently, illegitimate children and 'common law' wives have been able to claim, if they could prove they were normally supported by the deceased. This is a difficult matter if the man covers his tracks well or used a fictitious name. Ladies with children of assorted parentage were unlikely to succeed.

Making an abstract of a will

Wills of the nineteenth century were written without internal punctuation except full stops, which makes them look daunting. But they can be broken up into comprehensible chunks and reduced vastly in size:

'. . . I give and bequeath to my dearly beloved wife Martha Jane Toogood all that my freehold messuage and tenement known by the name of the Limes Acacia Avenue Southern Road in the parish of Croynge in the county of Surrey with all appurtenances thereunto belonging and I also give and bequeath to the aforesaid Martha Jane Toogood all that paddock adjoining unto the aforesaid messuage and tenement containing half an acre of land and also to the aforesaid Martha Jane Toogood all those my four freehold cottages situated at and formerly known by the name of Nos. 37 to 50 Gasworks Alley and now or lately known as Nos. 50 to 56 Dawkins Road in the parish of Stockham in the aforesaid county all of which premises aforesaid to remain to the aforesaid Martha Jane Toogood during her natural life provided always that she remain my widow and from the date of her decease or inter-marriage with any other husband I give and Bequeath the aforesaid messuage and tenement known as the Limes Acacia Avenue Croynge and also the aforementioned appurtenances thereunto and also the paddock adjoining the aforesaid premises containing half an acre and all those freehold cottages known formerly as Nos. 37 to 50 Gasworks Alley and now or late as Nos. 50 to 56 Dawkins Road Stockham aforesaid to my eldest son Josiah Mutch Toogood to have and to hold for him and his heirs forever provided that he pays out of the proceeds of the aforesaid messuage or tenement, paddock and four freehold cottages theretofore above more exactly described the undermentioned sums of money to his sisters hereinafter named that is to say to my daughter Mary Ann Martha Toogood the sum of one hundred and fifty pounds and to my daughter Eliza Jane Spratt the wife of John Spratt ironmonger and oil and colourman of Poynders Lane in the parish of Croynge aforesaid the sum of fifty pounds and to my daughter Sarah Ann Gubbins widow late the wife of George Gubbins horticultural sundriesman of Stockham High Road the sum of fifty pounds likewise within six months of the day when he shall take possession of the premises aforesaid after the decease or intermarriage of his aforesaid mother Martha Jane Toogood whichever shall happen first provided always that if the aforesaid Mary Ann Martha Toogood shall happen to die before the decease or intermarriage of my aforesaid wife

Martha Jane Toogood then the sum of one hundred and fifty pounds heretofore given to the aforesaid Mary Ann Martha shall remain to her lawful child or children if she die possessed of any such to any son or sons that attain the age of twenty one years or to any daughter or daughters that shall attain the age of twenty one years or shall marry before that age with the consent and approbation of my son Josiah Mutch Toogood their uncle in equal portions share and share alike but failing such issue lawful that the aforesaid sum shall remain and be given to my aforesaid son Josiah Mutch Toogood and to my daughter Eliza Jane Spratt and to my daughter Sarah Ann Gubbins and to my son Henry Knott Toogood in equal shares to such of them as shall be living. And as to the sum of fifty pounds above bequeathed to my daughter Eliza Jane Spratt if she should happen to die before the said legacy become due and payable then I give and bequeath the aforesaid fifty pounds to the child or children of the aforesaid Eliza Jane Spratt then living at the date when the aforesaid Josiah Mutch Toogood shall take possession of the said premises to any child or children being a son at the age of twenty one and to any child or children being daughters at the age of twenty one or shall marry first with the consent and approbation of my son Josiah Mutch Toogood their uncle in equal shares. And as to the fifty pounds bequeathed to my daughter Sarah Ann Gubbins widow aforesaid if she should happen to die before the said legacy shall become due and payable then I give and bequeath the said fifty pounds to my aforesaid son Josiah Mutch Toogood and my daughter Eliza Jane Spratt or the survivor of them in equal shares. To Elizabeth Jane Toogood the wife of my son Henry Knott Toogood I bequeath the sum of six shillings per week to be paid into her own hand by my son Josiah Mutch Toogood at his discretion and the aforesaid sum is not to be charged with any debt or incumbrance of her aforesaid husband my son Henry Knott Toogood for her lifetime while she remain my son's wife or widow and not after that and if she happen to die or being a widow to remarry with any other man then the aforesaid sum of six shillings per week is to be laid out by my aforesaid son Josiah Mutch Toogood for the maintenance and benefit of Henry Wilbe Toogood my grandson until he attains the age of twenty one. To my aforesaid grandson Henry Wilbe Toogood the sum of one hundred and fifty pounds when he shall attain the age of twenty one years and I earnestly entreat him that he shall at all times take the counsel and advice of his uncle Josiah Mutch Toogood as to his advancement in life . . .'

This can be reduced to:

'To d.b. wife MARTHA JANE TOOGOOD, my residence, The Limes, Acacia Ave., Croynge, Sy, plus paddock ½acre adj. plus 4 freehold cottages ex 37–50 Gasworks Alley now 50–56 Dawkins Rd, Stockham, Sy, for life while widow.
Rem on death or marriage to eldest son JOSIAH MUTCH TOO-

GOOD on condn. he pays to his sisters as foll:
to my dau MARY ANN MARTHA TOOGOOD, £150
to my dau ELIZA JANE SPRATT wife of JOHN S. ironmonger +
   oil & colourman, Poynders Lane, Croynge, £50
to my dau SARAH ANN GUBBINS wid of GEORGE G. hortic.
   sundriesman of Stockham High Rd, £50
If MAMT dies pre payt, then to legit issue sons 21, daus 21 or marr
   with consent of JMT or if d.s.l.p. rem. to JMT, EJS, SAG and my
   son HENRY KNOTT TOOGOOD, = shares ben. surv.
If EJS dies pre payt, then to living issue, sons 21, daus 21 or marr
   consent JMT
If SAG dies pre payt, rem. to JMT, EJS, = shares ben.surv.
To ELIZABETH JANE wife of my son HKT 6 sh per week, paid to her
   by JMT "not chargeable with debts of HKT" for life while marr to
   HKT or his widow. If d or re-mar then 6 sh per wk to her son HENRY
   WILBE TOOGOOD for maint & ben while under 21. At 21 HWT to
   have £150, "earnestly entreat him at all times to take counsel and
   advice of uncle JMT as to his advancement in life".'

Write all names in full the first time, then the initials, unless two
legatees have the same. Include the surnames of daughters, to show
which are married at the time of making the will. Indicate relationships
clearly – 'my dau', 'his dau', not just 'dau'. Note the type, amount and
limitations of legacies and what happens if it lapses. List all addresses –
to help census and other searches – including those of people apparently
unrelated, who may turn out to be aunties. Copy lists of items specifically bequeathed – individual pieces of furniture, portraits, etc, may
still be around, and a good list will give you an idea of the standard of
living at least. Copy verbatim any odd remarks or phrases which do not
immediately make sense, or comments which throw light on family
relationships.

Note the names of executor(s) and residuary legatees and the date of
will and codicils if any.

Useful abbreviations

If 'X' d.s.p. (or d.s.l.p.) = if 'X' dies without issue, or without
   legitimate issue.
21 or marr. = at the age of 21 or marriage before that.
rem. = remainder, what happens to the legacy when someone dies or
   another limitation happens.
= shares: in equal shares, share and share alike.
ben. surv. = benefit of survivorship, so if one of a group of named
   persons dies, the rest get it.
exor., exix. = executor, executrix.
resid. = all the residue of an estate not otherwise bequeathed in detail.

trustee(s) = person/s appointed *on trust* to carry out certain provisions, often long term in action. Trustees are governed by strict laws and may not invest in speculative schemes ('approved stocks' may be mentioned) or benefit from the trust monies.

per stirpes = by descent. A share which would have gone to a deceased parent is shared by all the children equally, however many there are.

hotchpot = the total value of the estate which is to be divided between heirs. Advances already made can be treated as part of this.

It isn't there!

A will may not be proved in the year the person died, so look onwards – it may take years to settle an estate. In the last century, if a widow and young children were left, there may have been no need to go to probate till the children were adult. An older widow with adult children comfortably established might succeed without formality and probate would come when she died, possibly twenty years later. Small estates could be passed on without attracting estate duty, so wills may not have been made or proved formally.

There may be no will for a person who was affluent in life. He – especially she – may have been enjoying life interests and annuities, which left no disposable estate. Look for the wills of the older generation of the family to establish this. Before 1890, some family estates were controlled by marriage settlements and later by family trusts, which operated like a life interest.

Copies and postal applications

A photocopy can be ordered in person at Somerset House for 25p a sheet, but this is not an on the spot service. You can also ask by post for a search, if you know the name, location and date of death within a year or so. They will search three years and let you know the cost of copying, with a minimum fee of £2. Write to Postal Applications, York Probate Registry, Duncombe Place, York TO1 2EA. They locate the entry, work out where the original is and obtain a copy (if possible) from the local registry or Somerset House. It is therefore not a rapid service, taking 3–4 weeks at the moment. They have no facilities for general searches at York now, though this may be possible in the future.

District Probate Registries

There are thirty District Probate Registries and sub-registries distributed throughout England and Wales where local executors could prove wills, though they could also use the Principal Probate Registry in London. (In the 1940s, the PPR was evacuated to Llandaff, hence some surprises for totally un-Welsh families). Each local registry was issued with a set of indexes for the whole country, which they may still hold.

Local registries never held copies of wills outside their own area and several have recently transferred even their own older wills to the local County Record Office (where they can be seen) or to the P.R.O. at Hayes (normally unavailable). Registries are not geared to protracted searches; even if they have the indexes, they may be reluctant.

They cannot make long postal searches for you, but if you are sure a will was proved locally, within the last 50 years, and have an exact date, they may be able to provide a photostat – but not of very large or awkward shaped wills. Normally copies should be sought in London or by post from York.

Most of the *older General Indexes*, to 1929 or 1940, have been transferred to local Record Offices, or may be in the future. Facilities for general search should be better there. Local *copy wills* to 1930 or 1940 may also be at the CRO, even when originals have been handed over to the PRO.

The location of present District Probate Registries and Sub-Registries is given below. DPR TOWN = local registry. (Exact addresses in phone book) Contact them to find out precise holdings and hours of opening. No Reg. = no DPR in county, nearest stated. *Ind* = earlier national indexes to 1929 or 1939 and location of nearest set. *Copy* = copies of wills, to the stated date, proved locally or for stated local areas. *orig* = originals of wills proved at local registry only.

Avon: (1974+) DPR BRISTOL. *Orig* to 1927 PRO; for Bristol + Bath 1927+at DPR. *Ind* + *copy* for Bath, Bristol to 1940 at Bristol CRO.

Beds: no Reg. *Ind* Beds CRO. *Copy* to 1930 Northampton CRO.

Berks, Bucks: no Regs. *Ind* at Oxford Bodleian (fee) or London.

Cambs: DPR PETERBOROUGH for Cambs, Hunts, pt Northants. *Ind* Cambridge RO. *Copy* to 1926 Northants RO.

Cheshire: DPR CHESTER has *orig*. *Ind* + *copy* to 1926 County, to 1940 City at Cheshire RO.

Cornwall: DPsR BODMIN has *orig*. *Ind* + *copy* to 1927 (Cty) at CRO Truro.

Cumbria: DPsR CARLISLE. no **orig**; *Ind* + *copy* to 1926 CRO Carlisle.

Derbyshire: no Reg. DPR Stoke, DPR Birmingham. *Ind* Birmingham Ref Lib, Nottingham CRO. *copy* to 1928 CRO Matlock.

Devon: DPsR EXETER has *Ind* but ? going to CRO Exeter.

Dorset: No Reg. *copy* (pr. Blandford) to 1940 at Dorset CRO, *Ind* CRO Bristol, CRO Hants, CRO Exeter.

Durham: No Reg. DPR Newcastle. *Copy* to 1940 Dept of Palaeography, Univ., Durham. *Orig* DPR York.

Essex: No Reg. DPR Ipswich. *Ind* + *copy* (N Essex only) to 1940 at CRO Ipswich.

Gloucester: DPR GLOUCESTER. *Ind* + *copy* (Glos) to 1940 at CRO Gloucester (fee £2 a day); *copy* (Bristol + Bath) to 1940 at CRO Bristol. *orig* to 1926 at PRO; 1926 + DPR Bristol.

Hampshire: DPR WINCHESTER. *Ind* + *copy* to 1940 at CRO.

Hereford: No Reg. *Ind* to 1935 CRO Hereford. *copy* (bound with Brecon, Radnor) to 1928 at Aberystwyth.

Hertford: No Reg. once pt of Peterborough district. *Ind* Cambridge, London. *Copy* (pt) Northampton RO.

Hunts: No Reg. DPR Peterborough. *copy* to 1940 at Northampton RO. *Ind* Cambridge RO.

Kent: DPR MAIDSTONE. *Ind* E Sussex RO Lewes or London.

Lancashire: DPR MANCHESTER, DPR LIVERPOOL, DPsR LANCASTER. *Ind* CRO Manchester, CRO Preston, CRO Liverpool. *Copy* to 1940 for Liverpool + Lancaster at Preston RO. Copy for Manchester, Salford at PRO Hayes. *Orig* local 1941–69 DPsR Lancaster; *Orig* local 1941 + DPR Manchester.

Leicester: DPR LEICESTER. *Ind* + *copy* to 1940 at CRO. *Orig* some at DPR.

London + Middlesex: at Somerset House.

Norfolk: DPR NORWICH. *Ind* Ref Lib; *copy* Norwich RO (NB fire damaged 1994, enquire).

Northampton: DPR PETERBOROUGH. *Ind* Cambs RO, Huntingdon; Birmingham Lib; Leicester RO; *copy* for Peterboro to 1940, local to 1930, some Herts, Cambs at CRO Northampton. *Orig* DPR Birmingham.

Northumberland: DPR NEWCASTLE. *Ind* DPsR York. *copy* for Newcastle + area at CRO Northumberland. *orig* 1928 + DPR.

Nottingham: *Ind* + *copy* to 1940 CRO Nottingham.

Oxford: DPR OXFORD, covers OXF, BKM, BRK. *Ind* Bodleian Lib, (fee for use) or London. *orig* + *copy* none pre 1973 at DPR.

Rutland: DPR LEICESTER *Ind* + *copy* to 1940 CRO Leicester. *Orig* DPR Leicester.

Shropshire: No Reg. DPR Chester. *Ind* Birmingham Ref Lib, CRO Chester. *copy* to 1940 CRO Shrewsbury. *Orig* 1930–42 DPR.

Somerset: No Reg. DPR Bristol, DPsR Exeter. *Ind* CRO Bristol, Exeter Lib. *orig* to 1926 PRO; 1927 + DPR Bristol.

Staffordshire: DPR STOKE ON TRENT *Ind* Birmingham Lib, CRO Notts. *copy* for Lichfield to 1930 ar CRO Lichfield. *orig* DPR Birmingham.

Suffolk: DPR IPSWICH. *Ind* DPR Norwich. *copy* to 1940 (local) CRO Ipswich; (local) CRO Bury St Edmunds.

Surrey: No Reg. – as London.

Sussex DPR BRIGHTON: *Ind* CRO Lewes, CRO Winchester; *copy* Chichester to 1940 at W Sussex RO.

Warwickshire: DPR BIRMINGHAM: *Ind* + *copy* local to 1940 at Birmingham Ref Lib; *Orig* DPR Birmingham (**West Midlands** see also Staffs, Worcs).

Westmorland: No Reg – DPR Carlisle – see Cumberland.

Wiltshire: No Reg. DPR Bristol. *Ind* CRO Bristol, CRO Winchester, *copy* to 1940 for Salisbury at CRO Trowbridge.

Worcestershire: No Reg – DPR Birmingham. *Ind* Birmingham Ref Lib. *copy* local to 1930 at CRO Worcester (TS index SOG): *orig* DPR.

Yorkshire: DPsR YORK, DPR LEEDS, DPR SHEFFIELD, DPR HULL, DPR MIDDLESBOROUGH. *Ind* CRO Sheffield, CRO Wakefield, DPsR York (not yet accessible); *copy* N + E Ridings to 1940 ar CRO Northallerton; W Riding to 1940 at CRO Wakefield; *Orig* proved York, Wakefield, Durham at DPsR York.

Isle of Man: Probate Ct Records at Probate Reg. Douglas, IOM.

Channel Islands: *Jersey* at Judicial Greffe, Royal Court, Jersey. *Guernsey* Ct of Dean of Guernsey, New St, St Peter Port, (real estate from 1841 for Guernsey handled by The Greffe, Royal Court, Guernsey.)

Wales

DPR for Wales LLANDAFF, DPR BANGOR, DPR CAERNARFON: *Ind* at Aberystwyth Nat Lib, CRO Carmarthen, CRO Caernarfon, CRO Cardiff, CRO Ruthin, CRO Cheshire. *copy* wills for all Welsh counties except Montgomery at Nat. Lib., Aberystwyth (Reader's ticket in advance required); *copy* for Montgomery at CRO Shrewsbury. Hereford wills (bound with Brecon, Radnor) also retained at Aberystwyth. *orig* for Bangor + St Asaph at DPR Bangor

Scotland

Wills proved locally at Sheriff Court were normally rapidly handed over to Register House, Edinburgh. There is a printed consolidated Index from 1876 in Legal Search Room there. *Wills* from 1823–65 or part may still be in Sheriffs' Courts or handed over. Consult *Scottish Record Office, PO Box 26, Edinburgh EH1 3YY* for details of location. List of Sheriff Courts + parishes they cover printed in *Scottish Law Directory*. Some consolidated district indexes – *Lothians 1823–65; Argyle, Bute, Dunbarton, Lanark, Renfrew 1846–65*; *Rest of Scotland 1846– 67* – accessible via LDS FHCs.

Ireland

Wills proved pre-1903 held in Four Courts, Dublin, were destroyed by fire and explosion in 1916. No *orig* survive for Principal Reg. Dublin, Meath, Kildare, Wicklow + pt of Kings Co survive. Many Wills Books for other counties in District Registries. *Gen Index of Grants* survives in PRO Ireland and all District Regs, which gives basic details of testator and exors. Surviving *pre-1922 records* for Belfast, Armagh, Londonderry (inc. Louth, Monaghan, Donegal in Eire) at PRONI Belfast; rest are in PRO Dublin. All post 1922 wills in correct PRO + District Registry.

Resealed Scots and Irish wills

Wills of Scots or Irish persons with some property in England or Wales had to be re-sealed in London and are therefore listed in General Indexes. From 1858–1876 these resealed wills are listed after Z.

Dominion wills

If any British person dying abroad or in any part of the Empire had any property in England or Wales, the wills had to be resealed in London, or in Edinburgh if the property was in Scotland. They are therefore included in the General Indexes.

PARISH REGISTERS

Why not use parish registers instead?

Instead of buying all these expensive certificates, why can't I get it all from parish registers? The usual problem is that by no means everyone went to church. After 1900, it becomes increasingly rare for all family events to be found dutifully recorded in one church, even in the country, and townsfolk are even less likely to be found. A lot of marriages took place in church, even if the couple never attended, but sometimes it wasn't the local one, but selected as a pretty backdrop for the dresses.

If you are quite sure your family were churchwardens to a man, then it may be worth trying this source, if it is easily accessible, but don't make undue efforts and risk disappointment and expense. My grand-parents were pillars of the local church when I was a child – but Grandfather, the churchwarden, was born Methodist, and Granny came from a Baptist family. Further back, both sides were church, but that first step of tracing their baptisms in parish registers, even knowing the two correct places of birth, would have been impossible.

If the registers are still in the parish, access may be diffifficult to arrange, though legally you are entitled to see them 'at any reasonable time' by prior arrangement; you may not be allowed to handle the registers personally, which leaves you dependent on another's care and skill: quite high fees can be charged per hour (£5 for the first hour). You may find nothing after an expensive trip.

Most registers are (or should be) deposited in the local County or City Record Ofice, where they can generally be seen freely. At least you don't lose money. But if you rely on the family's having been in the place where Father was born for ever, you could be disappointed. First do your homework, and find out several parishes where .the family definitely lived, from official certificates, censuses, wills etc. If these confirm that the family were resident in a particular county, in certain known places, then is the time to try parish registers.

The Victorian Parish Registers

Most people in 1837 probably did attend some form of religious worship, at least off and on. In villages, this is more correct than in towns, where family pressures and church-associated charity were less common. But church attendance fell off slowly during the century, and sharply in the present century, and in most places a variety of chapels competed very successfully for the faithful. Town populations multiplied enormously, and new parishes were created to accommodate the expected large congregations, so that in London and the great industrial cities, you will be faced with a choice of several sets of registers, even if you know for sure that your ancestors were Anglicans. The last century was a time of great mobility, so that a long search in one place may throw up one baptism – before they move to the next parish or town. If you discover from the censuses that your ancestors were born in a named rural area, that is a far better bet, but even then, your lot may be conspicuous by their absence from the church registers, because they were the only Bible Christians in the district and walked twenty miles every Sunday to worship. Chapel registers are by no means as easy to come by, after 1837, in general.

Assuming that your family were good Church of England folk, and stayed in one place, will the registers give you all you need? Possibly not, since the amount of detail is not the same as in certificates.

Marriage registers after 1st July 1837 do give exactly the same information. There are two entries to a page, identical in form with certificates. They will tell you the *names of groom and bride*; the *ages*, exact or 'full', meaning 21 or more; the *marital status*; the *occupation*, of the groom at least; the *place of residence*, which may be just 'of this parish'; the *name and occupation of the two fathers*. You also get the actual signatures (or marks) of the couple and their witnesses. However, you cannot legally photocopy the entries for less than £5, as agreed by the Registrar General. Most Record Offices will permit a photograph, however.

The snag is that marriages do not necessarily take place where the couple later lived. It was common to marry in the bride's home parish, or where she was working at the time. You could search for years for a Hampshire couple who happened to marry in London or Gloucester. National registration gets over this problem with a consolidated index for the whole of England and Wales from 1837 (with a similar Scottish index from 1855 and an Irish (Protestant) one from 1845).

Baptism and Burial registers show less detail than the equivalent certificates of birth and death. You can judge if this matters.

Baptismal entries probably will not show the date of birth, and baptism may be much delayed. They also very rarely indeed show the maiden name of the mother. You may have it from other sources, but things can get confusing if there are two John and Mary Smiths, or if one man marries two wives of the same name in succession. Carefully cross-checking with burial registers and censuses is necessary.

However, some births in the earlier years of registration (and even later in cities) were never officially notified, so that the census and baptismal entries are the only evidence of existence. Parish register entries are accepted as proof of age for pensions purposes therefore, and parents who left it late lose their offspring money. The unbaptised have to rely on tracing midwives in their nineties, or finding certain other documentary evidence.

Burial registers do not give the precise date of death, the marital status, occupation, cause of death, or the name of the informant (a probable relative). They do give *ages* – not necessarily accurate, nor the same as the certificate age. As a bonus, they may state the normal address or parish of someone who happens to die while visiting a daughter – which a certificate in England would not. If the death was violent or sudden, the register should note 'by coroner's order' which will alert you to look for an inquest report in the local paper.

Unless you come from a family of zealous churchgoers, the value of parish registers to you will diminish as the century wears on. Searching a city parish, or several of them, is a very time-consuming business. A combination of certificates and censuses can take you more rapidly back to 1837, and it is before this that the parish registers may become your prime source.

NEWSPAPERS

Local newspaper files

You can discover which newspapers were circulating in the ancestral neighbourhood from the CRO or reference library. In many cases, they have files at least of some of them, possibly on microfilm. The newspapers still in circulation, perhaps under another name, and their head office address, will be found in *Willing's Press Guide* found in most good libraries. There is a list of papers by county and town, so you can guess which circulated in a village nearby (or ask locally). Some newspaper offices will allow you to use their files, but don't go on make-up or press day, the two days pre-publication.

All British newspapers, and quite a lot from other places all over the world, are kept at the British Library Newspaper Library, Colindale Avenue, NW1. This is open on weekdays and Saturdays and free of access.

'National' papers in the modern sense were scarcely practicable until the railway network made rapid distribution possible. There were London newspapers, catering for local residents 'of the better sort', who could afford to buy them, with political, international, court and social news, and a ladle of crime. Until the 1850s, papers were very small and had no space for ordinary doings. Gradually, as taxes on paper and printing were removed, the size increased, but the market was still the upper and middle classes, though an occasional in-depth report on the plight of some particular section of London's poor was included. What happened outside London, if it did not involve the Royal family, the gentry or a good juicy crime, was not news. These London papers did have a limited, and delayed, circulation in the country, via gentlemen who had them sent down to their country houses, read them at leisure and then sometimes allowed the butler to take them to the local pub and read selected items to the rustics.

The provincial papers were few in number before 1830, and at first served the function of retailing old news from the London papers, then the speeches and doings of local gentry, and last other local events. The major events covered were those of interest to the likely readers, who were generally male and well to do. These were farmers' dinners, fat stock prices, the progress of railway building, municipal ceremonies and really steamy stories of sex and violence. Females were not catered for and their fathers or husbands were expected to keep the papers from them. London suburban papers, on the same lines as provincials, developed from the mid-1800s, though with less international and national news, because the 'Londons' were more available.

Gradually, international news was almost eliminated and national news was much reduced in the provincials, unless it had a local angle – much as nowadays. (*Weston couple's niece almost travelled on doomed coach.*) The gap was filled by increasing news of local events and people, until this predominated, and the later the paper was founded, the more likely it is to concentrate on purely local matters from the start.

What you will find in newspapers varies in different periods. Very few indeed have any sort of index yet, and there is a lot of small print to wade through, so the most readily traceable events will be those you know from other sources. These tend to be births, marriages and deaths, crimes, public triumphs and personal celebrations like golden weddings.

In the last century, births will not be there for everyone, and tend to be laconic in phrasing – *to the wife of Mr J. Jones, a son* – no names, often no place. Marriages don't get the spread with photos for ordinary folk, till about the 'thirties, though gentry and farmers' offspring are well covered, and the successful sons of local families marrying at some distant place are often mentioned. It depends on the attitude to publicity of the family, or the fact that the local semi-amateur reporter lived next door.

Nowadays, almost any death will be reported, with a resumé of the career, funeral details, mourners, wreaths from distant kin, etc. Last century, only deaths of the more substantial citizens were reported as standard. However, if your ancestor was exceptionally old, exception-ally poor (*starved to death in hovel*), exceptionally fertile (*mother of sixteen*), or a known joker or eccentric, he may be there.

Anyone who died accidentally or suddenly in public should have at least a short para, and a murder or suicide will get the full treatment – the Victorians loved a bit of gore. If Grandfather was run over by a cart and had the mangled remains of his leg amputated before dying of loss of blood, every last word and action of the two or three days involved will be reported, including his wages, his employer's name, and his usual habits of temperance or otherwise.

Living to a hundred, or even eighty, was less common last century, so occasional listings were made. The chances of celebrating Golden Weddings were therefore reduced, so that these events, even where they concern 'ordinary' folk may be written up extensively. The occasion may be used for a review of the happenings during the person's life. I have seen a detailed description of the life and times of a farm labourer which includes the names and characters of gentry, farmers, shopkeepers and pub landlords he knew over sixty years. Elderly servants of the gentry or local midwives are well commemorated.

Crime reports

If your ancestors were involved in any major crime, you will probably have been told about it, in hushed whispers. Wherever it took place, a murder with mysterious connections, or really sordid circumstances, will probably have been reported with relish in all local papers, not just in the area where it occurred.

The reports paid little attention to the laws of libel and often unflattering physical descriptions of the accused, and comments on his previous behaviour and other matters quite unconnected with the present crime are included.

The same may apply to the accuser or witnesses, whose demeanour, dress or accent may be ridiculed, so that even a limited involvement in a crime can produce useful personal or family information.

Sometimes ancestral thefts or indulgence in drunkenness or physical violence come as a complete surprise, having been edited out of family memory. A gap of unusual length in the production of children should be closely checked, in case it conceals a term in jail, and a sudden drop in social status may have a similar cause.

There are also many minor crimes included, like driving carts without lights or name plates; obstructing the highway with mud or rubbish; playing dominoes for halfpennies in a pub; making a noise in the churchyard during divine service; and the ubiquitous poaching of rabbits.

All in all, a newspaper can give you some surprises, pleasant or unpleasant. At the very least, you will be able to get the feel of what was going on at the time when your ancestors lived in the place.

RECORDS AND RECORD OFFICES

Using a Record Office

In general, County Record Offices are in or near the County town. City
or Borough Record Offices may be in or associated with the major
library there. (The standard abbreviations which covers them is CRO.)
You can find out the addresses and locations from the Gibson Guide
'*Record Offices and Where to Find Them*'. If there is only one for the
County, then all the deposited parish registers (and a great deal else)
should be there. However, if there are several offices, first check that
what you want is where you expect it to be. Cities sometimes take in
registers from just outside, sometimes their 'local' registers were deposited elsewhere years before they opened, though they may have
obtained filmed copies.

Most Welsh church registers were originally collected in by the
National Library at Aberystwyth, and CROs are comparatively recent
there. Far more Welsh people attended chapel than church, though. All
the older Scottish parish registers to 1855 (OPRs) are in Edinburgh, in
the same complex, New Register House, where the certificates are kept.
There is a charge for daily access to the complex and all the many
goodies available. Some have been filmed and copies are becoming
available, for instance in the Aberdeen Family History Shop.

Irish parish registers are a special case. Most of the Church of Ireland
registers were gathered together in a Dublin building called the Four
Courts, where they were burnt in the troubles of 1922. Those which
survive were copies kept in some parishes, though the Belfast Public
Record Office has microfilms of most of those in its own area. Catholic
registers are still in the parishes (some filmed, and in Dublin), and

Presbyterian registers may be in the church or at the denominational library in Belfast. A list of all surviving registers, with first dates, is printed in Donal Begley's *Handbook of Irish Genealogy*.

Once you have worked out when you can go to the CRO, the next step is to make sure that they are open on that day. A few close on Mondays, and there are occasional dates, mainly Bank holidays, the days after holidays, and 'stocktaking' days in autumn or spring, when they are shut. It is best to book a seat in the search room – some CROs actually demand it, most advise it, since offices are generally small and a lot of people want to use them. Check that they have the actual registers you want – sometimes they are in the parish, sometimes vicars borrow them back for exhibitions, and sometimes the dates you want are in books still in use.

A number of CROs belong to an Archive Network, and have a Ticket system. This costs nothing, but you will have to fill in a form and produce some evidence of identity with your name and address on. A driving licence or pension book etc is fine (but a passport isn't). Lincoln and Oxford need 2 passport photographs and Birmingham a second item like a rates demand or gas bill. This is not the sort of thing most people carry around. If you write in advance, the exact kind of identification required should be stated. The reason for the restrictions is that CROs have irreplaceable material, some of it saleable in foreign parts, and there have been one or two incidents of theft. In far more cases, documents have been damaged by careless handling, and some means of banning uncaring, clumsy people is required.

Take sufficient notebooks or A4 paper with you – tiny sheets the size of loo paper may look neat but they are too soon filled and overfilled. There are useful prepared lined forms for the different sorts of record too, from Allen & Todd of Ramsbottom. Take a supply of pencils too, since CROs do not permit ink or biro near original documents. 3B or 4B pencils make the darkest mark with least effort, but wear down fast, so take a pencil sharpener. CROs provide sharpeners, but they always either chew pencils up or disintegrate when you touch them.

Most CROs want you to hand over your case (even handbags in one or two), so put all the papers you actually need in a transparent envelope or zipped plastic wallet, with your pencils. Eat a hearty breakfast, so you don't need to stop and hunt for a cafe unless you want to. Take a sandwich, perhaps, but don't eat anything in the search room, not even the smallest sweet. Of course, you can't smoke, and people who slip outside and come back reeking of it are none too popular.

Talk as little as possible in a low voice if you need to ask something. Folk who come in and pin the archivist to the wall with a blow by blow account of their searches to date disturb the others, and you get a feeling of unwelcome in the hillside. Write to the CRO first, by all means, with a summary of what you have found that is relevant to their area, not forgetting to include occupations, and saying what registers you want to consult. Ask if there are any special sources they can recommend which might assist you. They should know if anyone is working on a book about glassblowers or coffee-mill makers in their area, with a card index in umpteen boxes. Every CRO has a motley collection of books, manuscripts, maps and lists which might apply, and they know best what is available.

Do your homework first, of course. If you have read your background books, you will know that if any member of the family was an innkeeper or printer or butcher, there could be a licence. Better-off people have wills, pay taxes and appear on a lot of lists. If you know your ancestors worked for a particular gentry family, ask if there are estate papers for that family. Consult *Unpublished Personal Name Indexes in CROs* (Gibson) and see if they have anything relevant. The archivists should be able to tell you of anything special, but it is up to you to search it.

In the same way, it is a good idea to study handwriting before you tackle older registers. Always work back from more modern ones anyway, so you get familiar with the names involved. An archivist will help you read one or two difficult words, but not whole documents. He or she might tell you what a strange local term means or point you to a dictionary or glossary. If you find yourself really struggling with a will, get a photocopy and puzzle it out at leisure at home.

Draw up a neat A4 size family tree of what you know, with limited details, like year dates instead of full dates. Make yourself a shopping list of surnames which belong and what dates people ought to appear in certain parishes, if they were not lying in their teeth to the census enumerator. But don't be too positive. If Jane was 25 in 1851, she could be born from April 1825 to March 1826 – assuming she got her age right. Put 'c.' for circa, about or a question mark or both – *Jane Barry c 1825/ 6?* – then you won't reject the one that turns up in 1824 or 1827 out of hand.

Write down all the surnames you are researching and any names associated with them, for good measure. Witnesses to a wedding often turn out to be relatives, so put 'Henry Sprott wit. 1869' or 'Mary Timmins visitor 1871' and note them if they come up. If you have to stop to think if it was Sprott or Strutt, you've wasted time. Don't reject a name because it isn't spelled exactly the way you spell it now. Most people were semi-literate at best – if it sounds rite, it is Wright.

Your aim is to gather up all the entries you can in the time at your disposal. The further you are from home, the harder you need to concentrate – don't stop to analyse what you have found, but scribble, scribble. Aim to head your page with the name of the parish or source, and preferably the CRO reference for it. All their documents will have a number or letter and number sequence which describes that document alone. If they find you a special manuscript, note its reference and description, then another time you can ask for it correctly, not as 'a little bundle of papers with a bit of tape round' – they've got thousands of those.

Even if you search a manuscript and find nothing, note the reference and put 'nil Bloggs'. Otherwise, some bright spark might suggest it again, and even charge for searching it. Note what you have been looking for though. The parish might have no Bloggs, but when you find that there are Porters in the family, it could be worth searching again – there are dozens of those. If you only search certain dates (1845 to 1860), say so. And if you do a quick dash through a period at the end of the day, note 'rough run', and then it could be worth doing thoroughly some time.

Family Historian's Law – the last ten minutes of the day will be the time when you find the most important entry.

Rough record keeping

When you start, the temptation will be to buy a nice fat notebook in which you can keep all your researches together. That way, madness lies, for you will write things down as you come to them, census entries, directories, registers,, wills, all mixed, and soon you will be totally unable to find anything. You know it's there, but where is it?

It is best to keep the different things separate. One way of doing it is to have a series of thin notebooks, one for each source. Another is to use A4 sheets of paper which can then be punched with holes and separated out into different sections of a file, for census, registers, wills, directories etc. Eventually, you will graduate to a file for each source, then two or three files for some of the sources. Another still is to feed everything into a computer – but you can't always take your computer round with you, so you will have to collect on paper, and be able to retrieve the results.

For instance, when you are searching censuses, write the entries for different places and from 1851, 1861, 1871 etc on separate sheets. That way, you won't look at an age and make the wrong deductions for birth date. For parish registers, a thin book for each parish keeps the work together, and as the numbers grow, they can be filed in alphabetical order, in a box or file, or series of files.

You don't need a massive outlay all at once. The equipment, like the facts, can be collected piecemeal, and can be acquired as useful gifts from the family instead of deplorable ties or collections of soap. But if you decide from the first that there will eventually be a lot of paperwork, then you will allow for expansion, instead of starting on fiddly bits of mini-file paper and having to copy out the whole lot before it blows away.

Start out recording as you mean to go on. Dates should always be expressed with the months as three letters, not a figure. This is partly because at some stage, you may acquire an American cousin, and

Americans write day and month back to front, so 10-4-1928 is the 4th of October, not the 10th of April. It is also clearer, since several figures look very similar, as 1 and 7, but JAN and JUL are distinct. For most purposes, it helps to get into the habit of writing the year first, then the month, then the day, since the year is what you need to know first.

It saves time to use a standard set of abbreviations, of which the first you need are:

b = born   **m** = married and **d** = died   **c 1896** = about 1896

Soon you will need:

1914 Mar Q, 1899 Jun Q = event registered in the March quarter of 1914, June Quarter of 1899 (where you have the date, but no certificate).
M.I. = monumental inscription (on tombstone)   **bur** = buried
bap or **bp** (doesn't matter which, if consistent) = baptised
pr bp = private baptism   **RIC** = received into church
WILL dtd 1882 Jan 6 pr 1884 Dec 1 = will dated 1882 proved 1884
(1841) 30+ = in the census taken on 6 June 1841 he was 30–34
(1851) = in the census taken on 30 March 1851 it says that . . .
(1861) = in the census taken on 7 April 1861 it says that . . . etc
ag lab = agricultural labourer   **appr** = apprentice
Family Historians' Jargon:
St Catherine's = General Register Office, England & Wales
Somerset House = Principal Probate Office, England & Wales
CRO = County Record Office (or City/Diocesan/Borough R.O. loosely)
PRO = Public Record Office (Chancery Lane, Kew or Census Office)
SOG = Society of Genealogists
FHS = Family History Society
PR = Parish Register   **OPRs** = Old Parish Registers (Scotland)
BTs = Bishop's Transcripts (copies of parish registers)

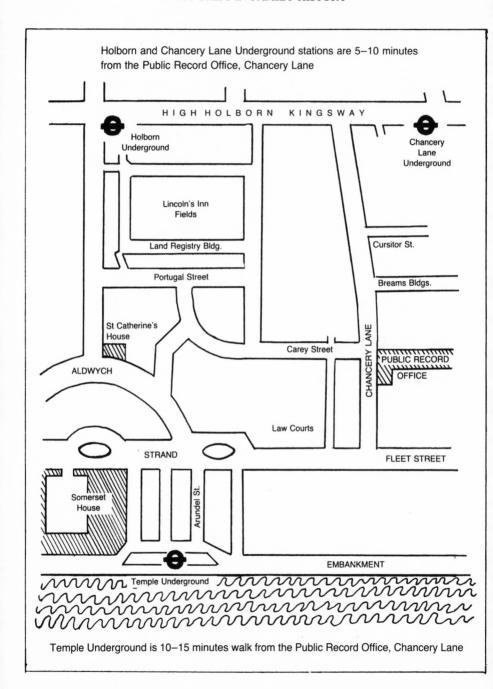

SELECTIVE BIBLIOGRAPHY

McLaughlin Guides

St Catherine's House
The Censuses 1841–81
Somserset House Wills
Wills Before 1858
Reading Old Handwriting
Annals of the Poor (to 1834)
Laying out a Pedigree
Nonconformist Ancestors
Using Manorial Records

No time for Family History?
Interviewing Elderly Relatives
Parish Registers
Family History from Newspapers
Simple Latin for Family Historians
The Poor Are Always With Us (Victorian Poor)
Making the Most of the I.G.I.
Quarter Sessions Records
Professions and Craft Trades

Gibson Guides (to location of records, listed by county)

Record Offices and How to Find Them
Census Returns 1841–91 in Microform (local copies)
Local Newspapers 1750–1920 (Eng & Wales)
Marriage, Census & Other Indexes
Simplified Guide to Probate Jurisdictions
Poor Law Records 1834+ (4 vols, Gazetteer & list of records by area/county)
Unpublished Name Indexes in CROs & Libraries
Local Census Listings (mostly pre-1841, some later)

Reference Books

1. *Main gentry/rich*
The Genealogist's Guide (G. Marshall 1903): A Genealogical Guide (J. B. Whitmore 1903–53): The Genealogist's guide
  (G. Barrow 1975): British Family Histories in Print (T. Thompson 1980).
Miscellanea Heraldica et Genealogica (This and several other periodicals have been surname indexed by Stuart Raymond)
Genealogists' Magazine (series)
Musgrave's Obituaries (to 1800)
Burke's Peerage; Burke's Landed Gentry: Burke's Knightage 1841
Hunter's Familium Minorum Gentium (v. minor gentry in north of England)
Visitation Pedigrees (various counties, not reliable)
County Families of (various counties 1860–1920 (E. Walford)
Burke's General Armoury (list of heraldic arms, not all genuine)
Fairbairn's Book of Crests (as used by various families)
Fox Davies' Heraldic Families (genuine only)
Scots Heraldry (Thomas Innes of Learney)
Simple Heraldry (Moncrieffe & Pottinger) fun and accurate
Dictionary of National Biography & supplements
Encyclopaedia Britannica (not latest edition)
Who's Who? (annual); Who Was Who? (1897–1959)

2. *Local to most counties*
Victoria County History (owners of manors, charities etc)
'Modern Domesday' list of property owners 1873 (may have whole country, or just local section)
County Record Society publications (local archie material)
Local learned or Archaeological Society publications
Directories; Pigott, Post Office, Kelly etc. various dates
Specialised county, town & village histories – consult Librarian
Extensive Bibliographies for many counties have been published in a series by Stuart Raymond

3. *National archive publications*
Harleian Society volumes (many parish registers, especially City of London, marriage licenses, Visitation pedigrees etc)
British Record Society volumes (indexes to wills etc)
List & Index Society volumes
Scottish Record Society volumes
Phillimore's Marriage Registers (most counties, selected parishes not entirely reliable)

4. *Professions and trades*
Alumni Oxonienses (list of students at Oxford University)
Alumni Cantabrigienses (students at Cambridge University)
Crockford's Clerical Directory (1858+)
Index Ecclesiasticus (J. Foster) (clergy 1800–40)
The Navy List (annual); The Army List (annual)
Naval Biographical Dictionary (W. O'Byrne 1849) (officers)
Dictionary of English Architects 1660–1840 (H. M. Colvin)
Dictionary of Music & Musicians (Sir George Grove 1954 ed)
Dictionary of British Sculptors 1660–1851 (R. Gunnis)
Biog. Dictionary of Railway Engineers (J. Marshall)
Was Your Grandfather a Railwayman? (T. Richards) rail archives

My Ancestor was a Merchant Seaman (Drs C. T. and M. J. Watts)
Location of Army Records (N. Holding)
World War One Army Records (Holding)
British Music Hall; Who's Who 1850 to 1975 (R. Busby)

5. *General genealogical sources*
Genealogical Research Directory, annual volumes
National Research Directory
Register of One Name Studies:
How to Start a One Name Group (D. Palgrave)
List of Non Parochial Registers deposited in the custody of the Registrar General 1841
Original Parish Registers in Record Offices & Libraries (+4 supplements) (Local Population Studies)
Cofresti Plywyf Cymru. Parish Registers of Wales (Williams)
Parish Registers, copies & Indexes: Inner London; Outer London; Nonconformists (Norman H. Graham)
National Index of Parish Registers (in progress, details of all registers in groups of counties) (Society of Genealogists)
Willing's Press Guide (current newspapers/dates started)
In Search of Scottish Ancestry (G. Hamilton-Edwards)
Scottish Roots (Alwyn Thomas)
Handbook of Irish Ancestry (Donal F. Begley)
The Irish Roots Guide (Tony MacCarthy)
My Ancestor was a Baptist (G. Breed)
My Ancestors were Congregationalists (D. Clifford)
My Ancestor was a Methodist (Wm Leary)
My Ancestors were English Presbyterians/Unitarians (Alan Ruston)
My Ancestors were Quakers (E. Milligan & M. Thomas)
Sources for Catholic and Jewish Ancestry (D. Steel)
Huguenot Society Transactions (registers etc of early Huguenots)
Homes of Family Names in Great Britain (H. B. Guppy)
Dictionary of Surnames/Origin of Surnames (Reaney)
Surnames of Scotland (G. F. Black)
Penguin Book of Surnames (B. Cottle)
Computers in Family History (D. Hawgood)

Useful Addresses

1. *London*
General Register Office (Office of Population, Censuses and Social Surveys), St Catherine's House, 10 Kingsway, WC2B 6JP
Principal Registry of Family Division, Somerset House, Strand WC2R 1LP (wills from 1858)
Public Record Office, Chancery Lane, WC2A 1LR (older records)
Public Record Office, Census Room, Portugal St, WC2A
Public Record Office, Ruskin Ave, Kew, Richmond TW9 5DU (newer records & services and colonial)
British Newspaper Library, Colindale Avenue London NW9 5HE
Guildhall Library, Aldermanbury, London EC2P 2EJ (also City of London RO)
Greater London Record Office, 40 Northampton Rd, London EC1R 0HB
Westminster Archives Dept., Victoria Library, Buckingham Palace Rd, SW1W 9UD
Borough Archive Depts: see list in *London Local Archives* (GLAN)
Society of Genealogists Library 14 Charterhouse Buildings, Goswell Road London EC1M 7BA (fee for use)
LDS Family History Centre, 64–68 Exhibition Road, Kensington W7
Guild of One Name Studies c/o Box G, 14 Charterhouse Buildings, Goswell Road London EC1M 7BA (post only)

Outside London
County and City Record Offices listed in Gibson Guide see Bibliography; several City Libraries have very large genealogical holdings inc.
Birmingham Central Library, Chamberlain Square Birmingham B3 3HQ
Liverpool Maritime Museum. Pierhead, Liverpool
Manchester Central Library, Archives Dept, St Peters Square, Manchester M2 5PD
National Library of Wales, Penglais, Aberystwyth, Dyfed holds the major archives for Wales
County Family History Societies via CRO/County Reference Library or write to (e.g. Beds) Family History Society c/o Federation of FHS, Benson Room, Birmingham & Midland Institute, Margaret Street, Birmingham B3 3BS
LDS Family History Centres all over country
Genealogical Society, Church of Latter Day Saints, 50 East North Temple Street, Salt Lake City, 84150, USA

Index